W0079547

The Wealth of Virtual Nations

Adam Crowley

The Wealth of Virtual Nations

Videogame Currencies

Adam Crowley
College of Science and Humanities
Husson University
Bangor, Maine, USA

ISBN 978-3-319-53245-5   ISBN 978-3-319-53246-2 (eBook)
DOI 10.1007/978-3-319-53246-2

Library of Congress Control Number: 2017934330

© The Editor(s) (if applicable) and The Author(s) 2017
This work is subject to copyright. All rights are solely and exclusively licensed by the Publisher, whether the whole or part of the material is concerned, specifically the rights of translation, reprinting, reuse of illustrations, recitation, broadcasting, reproduction on microfilms or in any other physical way, and transmission or information storage and retrieval, electronic adaptation, computer software, or by similar or dissimilar methodology now known or hereafter developed.
The use of general descriptive names, registered names, trademarks, service marks, etc. in this publication does not imply, even in the absence of a specific statement, that such names are exempt from the relevant protective laws and regulations and therefore free for general use.
The publisher, the authors and the editors are safe to assume that the advice and information in this book are believed to be true and accurate at the date of publication. Neither the publisher nor the authors or the editors give a warranty, express or implied, with respect to the material contained herein or for any errors or omissions that may have been made. The publisher remains neutral with regard to jurisdictional claims in published maps and institutional affiliations.

Cover illustration: Abstract Bricks and Shadows © Stephen Bonk/Fotolia.co.uk

Printed on acid-free paper

This Palgrave Macmillan imprint is published by Springer Nature
The registered company is Springer International Publishing AG
The registered company address is: Gewerbestrasse 11, 6330 Cham, Switzerland

For My Family

Acknowledgments

This book was made possible with the support and encouragement of many individuals. I am particularly indebted to my mentors: Demetres Tryphonopoulos, John C. Ball, Stephanie Gross, Patricia Bixel, David Haus, and Francis Hubbard. I also wish to thank several scholars associated with the Popular Culture Association/American Culture Association (PCA/ACA): Amy Green, Judd Ruggill, Matthew W. Kapell, Jule Schlag, Michele Brittany, Nicholas Diak, Jeffrey Cain, Ashley Barry, and Brett Butler. The University of Maine and its Honors College were also very helpful, and this work would not have been possible without the kindness and support of Jordan Labouff, Robert Glover, Sarah Harlan-Haughey, Joshua Roiland, Gregory Howard, Mimi Killinger, Mark Haggerty, Melissa Ladenheim, and François Amar. To Hannah Babcock, Abby Bellefleur, Haley Hunter, Ryan Lopes, and Dmitri Onishchuk—our classroom conversations were invaluable. My parents, Tim and Mary, and my brother, Steven, provided the guidance and support that brought this project to life, and I am deeply thankful for their encouragement. What is good and useful in this argument is good and useful because of the support I have received from these people. Anything that falls beyond these qualities in the following pages can be sourced directly to the author.

CONTENTS

Contents

CHAPTER 1

Introduction: Analyzing Wealth in Videogames

Abstract Crowley offers a much-needed consideration of how video-games represent capital. Focusing on the economic anxieties of the millennial period, Crowley draws attention to the functions of represented currencies in digital environments. As well as addressing the ways in which currency exchange facilitates the player's act of play, Crowley advances an analytical scheme for valuing wealth representations in videogames. "Analyzing Wealth in Videogames" concludes with an application of the proposed program to videogames and videogame theories significant to the period of the Global Great Recession.

Keywords Global Great Recession · Ken Levine, videogames · Wealth inequality · Income inequality · Edward Castronova

Select videogames from the period of the Global Great Recession (2007–2009) represent wealth and the wealthy as "surreal and mysterious entities."[1] Such and similar representations illustrate the surprising relevance of income and wealth inequality to videogame narratives and the player's act of play in the modern period, and indicate shifting values for the representation of capital in contemporary games with respect to historical representations. In surprising ways, these developments reveal and affirm the longstanding influence of a literary genre—the sentimental romance as defined by Northrup Frye—to the videogame form. This

© The Author(s) 2017
A. Crowley, *The Wealth of Virtual Nations,*
DOI 10.1007/978-3-319-53246-2_1

relationship can be inferred from the frequency with which acts of capital exchange contribute to themes of ascent and descent in numerous titles. Importantly, the relevance of key features of the sentimental romance—for instance, the hero's descent into an underworld—has already been noted by David M. Leeson in his consideration of pre-Great Recession examples of the first-person shooter.[2] However, and in ways Leeson could not have been expected to anticipate at the time of his writing, representations of wealth and the wealthy in titles from the period of the Global Great Recession and its immediate aftermath indicate that the videogame form has been informed by the ancient narrative curves and contours of sentimental romance for more than half a century.

With regards to the concept of form, this book stands on the notion that the videogame is appropriate for scholarly analysis because of its capacities for commenting on life as it is lived by players—or "gamers." A rationale for this notion can be inferred from independent arguments from Alexander Galloway and Edward Castronova. For his part, Galloway offers a consideration of what it is that makes videogames meaningful subjects for analysis in "Social Reality in Gaming."[3] There, he claims that videogames offer a novel form of "realism," one that facilitates specific actions that are relevant to the "social reality of the gamer."[4] The observation is noteworthy to the extent that it marks a very early effort to recognize something like a contextualizing loop between the videogame, the gamer, and the cultural conditions that inform these subjects.

Since the publication of "Social Realism in Gaming," theorists have analyzed these and related concerns from myriad perspectives and have worked to identify their salient features and interlocking concerns. Notably, significant work in this vein has emerged from scholars taken with the relevance of practical economics to videogames and gamers. Perhaps the best-known contributor to this burgeoning field is Edward Castronova. In *Synthetic Worlds: The Business and Culture of Online Games* and *Exodus to The Virtual World: How Online Fun Is Changing Reality*, he considers the various economic systems that tend to emerge during gameplay and contrasts these systems with their real-world sources. Importantly, he considers the practical limitations for representing social realities in videogame titles that are designed to entertain consumers in mass markets—a concept that Galloway anticipates but does not address in detail in his early work. Castronova considers the relevance of what he dubs "fun economies" to gaming worlds and player groups.[5] With reference to the literary tradition of the Horatio Alger rags-to-riches tale from the early twentieth century, Castronova argues that mass market video-games must avoid actual economic reality and instead produce a fantastical fun economy that "gives people a meaningful role in play," no matter who they may be in society. The fun economy, he contends, is necessarily constructed in such a way that players can "win" it: that is, acquire significant agency under the contextualizing rules for play afforded by such fantasy.[6] For Castronova, the compelling concern behind these cash-and-carry imaginary systems is an awareness that the actual economic conditions of daily life are simply not entertaining for most players.

Taken together, Galloway and Castronova's arguments define the videogame form as a digital, interactive entertainment with the capacity to address social reality, generally, and the economic anxieties of players, specifically. Certainly, there are serious and ongoing debates about the essential capacity of the videogame form to address complex cultural concerns. The notion is latent in Galloway's own work and has been explored in some detail by critics such as Amber Davisson and Danielle Ghem, who attend to the necessarily superficial experiential opportunities that are afforded to players as they play within supposedly realistic scenarios, where they are denied "harsh realities" and other pragmatic eventualities in favor of gamed content.[7] However, such capacity is—for the moment—not the primary concern of this argument: rather, here, attention is directed toward the form's potential for addressing a game designer's estimation of social reality and its relevance to the player's act of play.

With respect to capital and its representation, Galloway and Castronova's arguments can lead to the conclusion that any potential videogame commentary on an economic system is contingent upon the game's rhetorical situation: that is, the intentional (or potential) set of communications the title can convey to its audience (the player). As Marcus Schulzke notes, Galloway indicates as much when he observes that "virtual worlds are always in some basic way the expression of utopian desire," which requires a necessarily pared-down representation of reality capable of engaging the player in his or her respective situation.[8] Castronova reminds us that such selectivity is almost certainly doomed to compromise by larger market expectations bearing on the player's cultural positioning. However, the very notion that games can make meaning—compromised or otherwise—with a commentary on the economic realities of daily life is in and of itself indicative of the form's discursive capacities. In the special instance of represented capital, these capacities are themselves fascinating subjects for consideration, if for no other reason than a theory to account for their associations with capital beyond the experience of play has yet to be explored in detail, though the notion has certainly emerged in criticism, as is evident in Castronova's reflection on the emergence of "fun economies."

Indeed, Castronova is among the first to note that, while a given fun economy can eschew the harsher realities of a functional economy, it is not at all certain that any title and its attendant representations of capital can be divorced from these same realities. Indeed, it is to be expected that the game remains in a kind of ongoing conversation with the various markets that deliver the title to the player. Castronova points this out in *Exodus to the Virtual World*. Speaking of online, persistent videogames, he observes that a fun economy of even moderate complexity will require a contextualizing policy, one that will need to be enforced and regulated by ever-evolving, real-world businesses with roots in an actual economy.[9] He contends that this will lead to a clash of in-game and real-world interests over time, which will lead to a blurring between capital that is external to a fun economy with capital that is internal to that fun economy. The long-term functionality of such a game, he contends, is in large part dependent upon the mediation of these interests.

Related warnings about the functional limitations of represented capital arise in McKenzie Wark's *Gamer Theory*. Wark generally associates video-games with the economy of a "casino," that is—a fun economy by a different name, but one that is decidedly tipped in the favor of the entity that provides the fun, in the sense that it is designed to require more and more time and capital from the player as the experience of play (with its attendant representations of capital) persists.[10] Wark argues that this creates a conflict in which the player alternates "between merger with, and separation from, the [game]."[11] This view of the videogame form and its possible functions raises anxious questions about the limits of the player's agency in his or her act of play, and it also prescribes a nominal value for the role of capital in gameplay, representational or otherwise: for example, such representations assumedly facilitate in some manner the player's controlled, periodic merger with and separation from the game, however manifested and defined.

A similar determination is expressed in a work from the same period, Ian Bogost's *Persuasive Games: The Expressive Power of Videogames*. However, Bogost's claim is perhaps even more unnerving than Castronova or Wark's as it identifies a determinative feature of the videogame form that portends a reductive value for the representation of any subject. He argues that games actively try to influence "the player's relationship with [the game] by constraining the strategies that yield failure or success."[12] For Bogost, such constraining belies an "art of persuasion through rule-based representations and interactions," which he dubs "procedural rhetoric."[13] Certainly, Bogost is speaking with a grand and totalizing vision for the videogame form, one that should be broadly tested before it is embraced or rejected. With regards to the special subject of capital, this testing can proceed with a consideration of how such rule-based representations and interactions might incorporate representations of capital in one form or another to persuade gamers to one or more hypothetical positions.

Collectively, Castronova, Wark, and Bogost identify potential functions for the representation of capital in videogames that are supposedly specific to the videogame form. Such work anticipates a significant consideration of the representation of capital in games that begins with an essential question: namely, whether—and how—the representation of capital in videogames may affirm or otherwise comment on broader conceptions of capital: that is, specific conceptions that exceed the immediate conditions of play but which are informative of it. Thomas Piketty's work is exciting precisely because it provides a logical framework for valuing capital inside and outside of games, with respect to its assumed relevance for populations living under extraordinary levels of wealth and income inequality. His revolutionary statistical models, which work to illuminate the economic concerns of our time and the recent past against the seemingly inescapable realities of capital divergence, establish a detailed and practical worldview for calling so-called "fun economies" to account in terms of their broader social significance to the concept of capital itself. Indeed, Piketty's findings compel a specific question about the representation of capital, regardless of its medium of origin: when and where does it conform to data-driven assumptions about middle-class perceptions of wealth in the modern world?[14] Thanks to authors like Galloway, Castronova, Wark, and Bogost, it is reasonable to address the videogame form for its general relevance to such perceptions.

However, and before proceeding, it is important to note that the concept of represented capital in games necessarily stands on a basic assumption that such representations are part of a larger, contextualizing subject—shared between form manifestations—that imbues them with essential meaning. For the purposes of this investigation, that subject is "narrative," a term that has a very troubled history in scholarship on videogames, and in scholarship that makes use of videogames. The relevant discourse and its shortcomings are all too evident in the well-documented calamity now generally referred to as the "ludology versus narratology" debates.[15] Excellent assessments of this near field-wide failure have been produced in recent scholarship: for example, work from Matthew Wilhelm Kapell and Amy M. Green and others in *The Play Versus Story Divide in Game Studies*, and by Janet Murray in *The Last Word on Ludology v Narratology*. Thus, there is no need to rehash the various intellectual battles that initiated and sustained a false schism between these disciplines here. However, it is important to note that while Castronova, Wark, and Bogost's theories have many merits, they do not evince a significant understanding of narrative theory or narrative theories traditionally associated with narratology, the touchstone field for modern considerations of narrative in multimedia and transmedia subjects. Again, this is not a failure on the part of these critics and their respective academic interests *per se*, but it is a reality of their work and its intellectual context and trajectory, so it must be addressed.

It will be necessary to consider specific narratological concepts at select points in the following arguments. Perhaps the most significant such concept is the concept of "formal determination."[16] The term will be used as it is used by one of the more noteworthy figures from classical narratology, Gérard Genette. In his *Fiction and Diction*, Genette describes the concept as pertaining to an assumed constant rhetorical value that delineates the landscape in which a mode of discourse occurs. The concept is useful in conjunction with Genette's definition for "narrative" in *Narrative Discourse: An Essay in Method*, which is "the expansion of a verb."[17] Paired, they establish a fundamental and bounded position, which is that the narrative is a determining feature of the subject at hand—in this case, the representation of capital in videogames—and that, as such, it can be identified by the expansion (e.g., development) of a verb that is associated with the videogame, generally, and the title's evident features—for example, capital—specially.

Before offering a rationale for this conceptual pairing—or the verb, exchange, that will be associated with narrative—a field-first explanation of what narratology is should be considered, if for no other reason than to provide a timely explanation and demonstration of how the discipline might be approached and utilized. Part of this consideration will include examples of what can happen to criticism and commentary when narratological terms are used incorrectly or without aim by scholars, fans, and industry leaders. Once this view has been articulated, it will then be possible to talk about representations of capital in videogames as features of distinct acts of exchange in narratives, and to recognize them as part of the evolving stories we have told and are telling ourselves about wealth and the wealthy.

To begin at the beginning, the French term "*narratologie*" (narratology) was coined by Tzvetan Todorov in 1969 to denote a Saussurian "science of narrative."[18]Over the next decade, Todorov and several prominent French structuralists piloted this extension of Saussurian linguistics to diagram abstract narrative systems for a host of literary and commercial works. Such scholarship is now generally associated with the discipline's "classical" stage, which is widely regarded to culminate in Seymour Chatman's *Story and Discourse*, F. K. Stanzel's *A Theory of Narrative*, and Gérard Genette's *Narrative Discourse: An Essay in Method*. In *Narrative Fiction: Contemporary Poetics*, Shlomith Rimmon-Kenan indicates that the first major challenge to the classical Saussurian approach emerged in the form of deconstructionist literary analysis. Rimmon-Kenan characterizes the initial deconstructionist challenge to narratology with an assertion from J. Hillis Miller, who rails against "the systematic study of literature," condemning its "schematized rationality devoted to intellectual mastery."[19] Rimmon-Kenan and others responded to Miller's charge in the 1980s by calling for new investigations into the presumed schematic limitations of the major models that had come to define the field. More specifically, Rimmon-Kenan and others postulated that the nature of the presumed failings would become evident under analyses of the discrepancies within and between the major interpretive schemes, particularly when the models were divorced from their original contexts and applied to transmedia and multimedia subjects.

However, rather than expose the fallacies of the classical designs, such work would go on to inspire what David Herman identifies as the "narratological renaissance," a multimedia and multidiscipline leap forward that transpired during the ensuing decade.[20] The renaissance was marked by widespread interest in "rethinking the conceptual underpinnings" of the structuralist models to ascertain their proper "scope of applicability." One result of this work was the identification and elevation of key classical concepts—for example, focalizer, focalized, and analepsis (flashback)—across an ever-broadening range of subjects. A general effect of this movement was a near-simultaneous flowering of narrative theory's numerous branches, which produced and continue to produce "a profusion of new methodologies and research hypotheses...on the forms and function of narrative."[21]

Martin Kreiswirth explains that this work is both informative of and contextualized by a parallel and ongoing shift across the social sciences, a transition he dubs the "narrative turn."[22] This "turn" speaks to various endeavors to identify the potential roles of narration within and between the "legal, medical, psychological, and economic discourses," as well as other forms of cultural exchange. As Ansgar Nünning notes, these forays have been so productive and numerous, and their findings specified under so many disciplines, that the very term narratology has undergone a substantial revision.[23] Indeed, as early as the mid-1990s, many working within the field stopped using the word "narratology" and, instead, began to differentiate between "classical narratology" and "postclassical narratology."[24] The former concept indicates the discipline's longstanding and often intertwined Anglo-American, Continental, and Eurasian roots—which find their ultimate expression in the Saussurian models—while the latter term recognizes the many and varied global research agendas that have emerged from mixed media as well as sociological considerations of the classical constructs.

Notably, the classical and postclassical traditions are awash in competing and often irreconcilable definitions, including definitions for "narrative."[25] However, it is also true that what has been arguably the field's most productive classical model in the postclassical period—Gérard Genette's commentary in *Narrative Discourse: An Essay in Method*—and its associated definition for narrative have been translated by authors as diverse as Susan S. Lanser and Mieke Bal across a range of media and critical perspectives. Notably, these same and other critics have also made significant use of the attendant concepts Genette explores—for example, voice, person, tone, and order—to formalize their bounded, inter-, and intra-textual investigations.

This is the missing context behind what Janet H. Murray characterizes as the debate between select, self-affirmed ludologists within the digital storytelling community and their imaginary, straw-men "narratologist" antagonists.[26] It is merely, Murray explains, a one-sided argument, perpetuated by computer game formalists anxious to rebel against a poorly understood "thing that must be repudiated in order for their own interpretation to have meaning": that is, narratology. Such anxiety, Murray explains, is latent in early work from Espen Aarseth, who calls dismissively on narratologists to prove that "games are stories in a well-argued and defined way," and, until then, essentially remain silent about games. Aarseth's concern, per Murray, comes from his desire to study games as their own category of cultural object, with the intention of identifying their definitive features. However, and as Murray notes, no one has bothered to collect Aarseth's digital gauntlet and argue that there "is no difference between games and stories, or that games are merely a subset of stories."

While it is true that contemporary narratologists have shown little interest in Aarseth's challenge (and that the scholarly debate has cooled off considerably), it should be noted that Aarseth's anti-narrativist view is alive and well in the contemporary period, though it has become a battle cry in the popular press and on fan blogs, rather than in academic journals. Perhaps the best-known articulation of this concern is Clint Hocking's piece on so-called "ludonarrative dissonance."[27] The phrase, coined in 2007, rests on the assumption that while game and story elements can be divided into distinct categories, story elements must function in the service of a presumed organizing game dynamic, or the narrative will somehow "break [the game's] contract with the player" and create the experience of gameplay "dissonance." Hocking's primary example of such discord is drawn from the original *BioShock*, which he argues promises the player a gaming experience of Randian power acquisition through self-direction but denies the player the opportunity to acquire such power and self-direction with a complicating storyline.

Hocking's argument can be further aligned with Aarseth's challenge and the claims of other early game formalists, such as Gonzalo Frasca, based on its rhetoric. For example, Hocking does not provide specific definitions for any of his key concepts: for example, terms like "ludic" and "narrative." It is true that Hocking uses certain terms that have become associated with ludic—such as "game" and "play," and terms for "narrative," such as "story" and "fiction"—but he does not associate either category with any specific conception of either term. With regards to "narrative," such rhetoric is generally in keeping with the computer formalist arguments identified by Murray, many of which roundly reject critical approaches to narrative without advancing a specific conception for the term, to say nothing of the broader field of narratology. Certainly, by 2001 narratology was a term in need of qualification, thanks to the by that time well-established divisions between the classical and postclassical approaches. The essential lack of understanding about these developments within the computer game formalist community is evidence in foundational work from Gonzalo Frasca, who presents the term "ludol-ogy" and along the way simply asserts "narratology had to be invented to unify the works that scholars from different disciplines were doing about narrative."[28] The claim is confounding and essentially absurd to the extent that it fails to mention that such unification had a specific Saussurian directive and that it arises from a particular critical tradition with embedded, bounded assumptions. Moreover, it misses entirely the notion that the field has a real and by that time very well-established intellectual infrastructure.

In this context, it is noteworthy that no one has noticed that the conceptual categories that define Genette's scheme can deescalate the formalist fear that narratology will somehow lead to the notion that "there is no difference between games and stories, or that games are merely a subset of stories."[29] For instance, Genette is well aware that the association of "narrative" with a particular denotation immediately limits the scope and potential applicability of a critical program, and states as much at the beginning of his argument in *Narrative Discourse: An Essay in Method*[30] and affirms this notion again with his commentary on formal determinations in *Fiction and Diction*.[31] Indeed, Genette reminds us that criticism is intentionally never universal, and only ever meaningful to an elaboration of a given perspective's essential assumptions. In short, from a critical perspective to say that "games and stories are the same" is mean-ingless because narratological terms (e.g., formal determinations) would only address an aspect or potential interpretation of games and stories in the context of a bounded scheme.

However, it should be noted that Genette's very definition for narrative—that is, the expansion of a verb—holds novel potential for the analysis of games. This action-oriented term enables the critic to assess a title's elements as existing in a dialectical relationship with the verb chosen for analysis. Under such study, this association would deter-mine the identified elements' specific as well as general relevance to the game in question, in the bounded context of the formal determination of narrative. It would also enable a consideration of their relevance to the game's overall presentation of the identified verb, and to that game's relationship with other games that enunciate the same or similar verbal concerns. For example, if this concept is applied to *BioShock*, the issue of whether the game's various elements create the experience of player dissonance is less significant than the question of how the game's features might relate to an organizing verb or verbs. To use Hocking's own language, the game is concerned with the player "seeking power" and "helping Atlas" overthrow Andrew Ryan.[32] Hocking then argues that the experience of play effectively curtails the player's ability to seek power in ways that are somehow aligned with the game's supposedly overarching commentary on Randian self-interest. This assumption places Hocking's never-actually-detailed conception of such self-interest at the heart of the game, where it becomes a silent adjudicator of player action and the critical standard for noting supposed dissonance. However, if the critic makes either "seeking" or "helping"—and let us go with "helping," though "seeking" is equally apt—the boundary concept for analysis, the various gameplay elements Hocking identifies in his argument are transformed from agents of dissonance to discrete developmental manifestations of the identified verb or verbs, and can be adjudicated for their evident contributions to such development as it emerges in the course of gameplay, rather than as evidence of a nebulous conceptual failure. For example, how do the player's compelled actions characterize or otherwise give shape to his or her larger experience of helping, both generally and within the context of particular moments? In answering this question, the critic would necessarily begin with the premise that the organizing concept—to help—is defined by the identified and associated game content, and not—like Randian self-interest—by an external set of assumptions that the game must somehow affirm or in its failure to affirm erroneously create the experience of dissonance. In this way, the critic might respect the game's various features for their individual and collective contributions to the player's act of play: for example, this is what it means to help in *BioShock*. In its conclusions, this work could define the particularities of such efforts—conflicted or otherwise—to the game's larger statement on helping, whatever it might be. Certainly, the significance of such analysis is necessarily limited by the critic's characterization of the game's evident processes for articulating verbal development. However, once identified, these processes could become a point for the comparison of individual works. Such analysis has the potential to detail how a pairing or collection of games might contribute to a general discourse on a verb or bounded set of verbs—and this is the first step for determining the possible relevance of discreet representations to the player's act of play within and between titles.

The history of narratology can do more than clarify some of the major debates haunting ludology. A specific example of how narratological concepts can contribute to the field can be found in an association of

Genette's program for analysis with a specific instance of terminological development in the game design community. For example, at the 2013 Game Developers Conference, the head of *Irrational Games* and developer of *BioShock*, Ken Levine, delivered an hour-long presentation entitled "Narrative Legos."[33] In the overview for the presentation, Levine claims that by "breaking narrative down into its smallest yet non-abstract elements and finding ways to combine and recombine them, one could potentially build a nearly infinite array of narrative opportunities out of these small building blocks." It is a fascinating claim and one that will sound familiar to critics conversant with classical narratology. For his part, Levine considers a hypothetical narrative structure that emerges through anticipated, select interactions between players and characters, such as the kind that can be found in titles like *Middle-earth: Shadow of Mordor* (2014).

Interestingly, Levine, like Aarseth, Hocking, and Frasca, does not provide a working definition for "narrative." However—and surprisingly—this is not a major issue in his presentation, which—and in seeming defiance of its name and overview materials—is not overly concerned with "narrative," regardless of the term's potential denotations or connotations. Rather, Levine spends most of his time detailing a plan for game design concerned with player agency in open-world environments. However, while Levine may not have a specific definition for the term, it is true that he uses it to a specific effect, and a consideration of that effect and its value in Levine's larger argument speaks to the quality of his vision, and the value of that vision to the project at hand.

The relevant statements emerge in the context of Levine's comments on "zero-sum" play experiences.[34] Per Levine, zero-sum play dynamics have "narrative" implications that can connect his vision of atomized storytelling components to a supposedly larger academic conversation that, he says, "smart people" are already having about videogames. Crucially, from the first, Levine uses the word "narrative" and phrase "linear narrative" interchangeably. With regards to his promise to identify the "smallest yet non-abstract elements" of narrative, this conflation raises questions about whether Levine associates such elements with both terms, or if they are more relevant to one of the terms than the other. While that essential question is never explicitly clarified in the presentation, it is true that Levine employs these terms in a consistent manner and in ways that eventually indicate their specific and unifying value. For example, he situates "narrative" and "linear narrative" games in a binary relationship with what he calls "system games." He claims that linear narrative games (e.g., *Thief, BioShock*) and system games (e.g., *Civilization, X-Com*) can be distinguished to the extent that in the former the decisions the player makes "don't make a difference at the end," while in the latter they do make a difference. With regards to the project at hand, these comments are fascinating, insofar as they indicate an awareness of narrative and its fundamental relationship with choice, and the ways in which this essential relationship precedes and exceeds the tropes of genre in at least the short list of titles implicated in Levine's presentation. Indeed, the relationship between narrative-as-such and player choice even exceeds the binary relationship Levine establishes, insofar as the logic of his comments indicates that narrative and choice are the determining factors that underlie his essential game categories. Consequently, the concepts and their relationships appear to be matters of form itself.

From this interesting position, Levine goes on to identify two additional categories of theoretical content that might be used to infuse otherwise zero-sum games with the storytelling indeterminacy that, he claims, has long been enjoyed by players of system games. Levine refers to these content categories as "Stars and Passions."[35] Stars, he says, are hypothetical "interactive AI personalities" that emerge during gameplay. He goes on to explain that stars have individual "Passions," or definitive desires that are transparent to the player and exist relative to player action. From this supposition, he explores a "zero-sum" model for gaming in which the player's act of play—his or her interaction with various Stars and other in-game features—has a continual and interconnected impact on the Passions of other Stars, in ways that modify subsequent Star engagement with, and evident attitudes toward, the player over time. In this way, Levine explains, the "replayability" of the hypothetical world is improved or increased, as there are manifold opportunities for the player to have a range of experiences depending on the status of the total Passions in the world at any given moment. It creates, he argues, an "X to the Y" number of possible experiences during zero-sum game play, and achieves the experiential possibilities of system games within the limited—though hypothetically vast—opportunities of what is technically still a zero-sum experience.

By its very suppositions, Levine's scheme raises interesting, hypothetical, and currently unresolved questions about the significance of choice to player action. For example, what does it mean for a zero-sum game to be "player driven"—the question takes on more urgency given the essential illusion of choice that is implied by Levine's scheme: for example, the player is presented with vast possibilities that are explicitly zero-sum, a fact that would seem to place enormous qualifications on what it means for the player to "drive" narrative development in the first place. Regarding the project at hand, "Narrative Legos" illuminates the need for further defini-tion of the assumed relationship between the narrative and the player's choices for play— which might be termed the act of play itself, insofar as such action can serves as the foundation and potential context for the player's decision-making opportunities, zero-sum or otherwise.

From this, it is possible to hypothesize the relevance of what Genette calls a "formal determination" for the player's act of play, a conceptual constant that delineates the landscape in which a discursive mode—in this case, the player's act of play—unfolds. Genette's definition for narrative provides one path for analysis, to the extent that it constrains the relation-ship between narrative and choice in Levine's comments to choices that are undertaken as part of a larger expansion or general development of a singular verb during play, or at the very least prioritizes such development as an investigative concern. Moreover, it leads to the focused considera-tion of choices that bear on a certain act, or what can be understood in terms of a certain act, whatever that act may be. Certainly, this association comes at considerable cost for analysis: it demands a focus on only one of what very well may be many equally significant actions that inform a given act of play. Nevertheless, it is a productive constraint for analysis to the extent that it establishes a formal concern that can then be considered for its relevance to a single game as well as multiple titles.

Given that the concept of choice is so broad, Levine's comments on the dynamic nature of Passions relative to Star interactions takes on special and crucial meaning for the project at hand. Considered as such, these collec-tive exchange opportunities affirm something like an exchange market with global consequences: for instance, certain choices lead to—as well as deny—other opportunities for choice for the player in his or her act of play. As such, the system Levine hypothesizes raises inherent questions about exchange value: for example, which exchanges between players and Stars will lead to the most or least accessible avenues for play, to say nothing of other potential paths of varying quality or qualities?

Questions about the illusion or reality of exchange opportunities to the player's experience of play have demonstrable thematic significance to Levine's own *BioShock Infinite*, a title that has special relevance for the project at hand due to its deep investment in representations of wealth and the wealthy as "surreal and mysterious entities." A consideration of the title as such can reveal the value of the proposed program of analysis to a title that carries in its narrative DNA the essential romantic concerns that have provided shape and meaning to exchange in videogames for over a half century.

BioShock Infinite presents literal as well as symbolic engagement with the twin market forces that underlie Piketty's grand scheme: convergence (wealth distribution) and divergence (wealth inequality), and the significance of these forces to emerging technologies. In Piketty's modeling, the act of divergence is more relevant to certain points in time than others. For example, he repeatedly identifies the pre-World War One European and Regan-era American epochs as moments of exceptional divergence with long-term significance for global markets.[36] Regarding the era of the Great War, Piketty considers the significance of battling land barons prior to the beginning of the great conflagration, who struggled with shifting land and labor values, which were disturbed by key technological developments that emerged beyond the bounds of established regulatory markets.[37] In Piketty's estimation, the markets of this period reacted with a grotesque expenditure of human capital to master those technologies and ensure continuing divergence in systems that then threatened the opposite, convergence. These forces, he explains, are also relevant to and have parallels in the contemporary American situation, beginning in the mid-1980s when the emergence of novel technologies once again upended established markets and were subsequently co-opted by corporate entities that used their newfound financial advantage to establish the modern corporate "supermanager."[38] While this transformation may not have resulted in the same kinds of death and destruction that came with the Great War, it has, Piketty explains, had the massive cultural effect of essentially arresting the American lower and middle classes in a perpetual state of economic limbo, while the rich have continued to prosper in quite literally unimaginable ways.

The moments in Piketty's scheme that denote these major cultural shifts toward divergence are significant to *BioShock Infinite*. Set largely in 1912, the game follows the adventure of Booker DeWitt in the cloud city of Columbia, where he travels under the careful observation of the city's mysterious creator, Rosalind Lutece, to find and capture Elizabeth Comstock, hoping to exchange Elizabeth to a shadowy figure to pay off a vague but assumedly profound debt. Along the way, he battles two particularly evil land and labor barons, who are bound by a shared—but deteriorating—Technocracy. At a key moment, the story diverts to 1984, to a version of New York that is in a state of dramatic economic and social upheaval with symbolic value to Piketty's statistical findings from the end of the century. These moments and their associated content are informed by the notion that the wealthy are determined to crush any potential challenge to their technological superiority and are willing to expend countless lives to maintain market divergence.

With regards to Piketty's argument that pre-War Europe was increasingly defined by isolated rural communities and growing urban centers of power and production, it is worth noting that Columbia is a city of distinct exchanges, all of which delimit certain aspects of labor and leisure in the game's landscape. For example, the city's "Raffle Square" sits at the heart of Colombia's consumer district; the city's beach area, "Battleship Bay," is a front for leisure activities of all sorts; the city's major museum, "The Hall of Heroes," has its own socioeconomic positioning, too. Similar differentiations exist in Columbia's proletarian quarters: the "Finkton Docks" are an isolated shipping area, the "Bull House" collects the city's police forces; and the "Shantytown" ghetto is where this city in the sky keeps its miserable unfortunates. The relevance of these isolated destinations to Piketty's scheme is further underscored by their literal convergence and divergence, as they are physically driven together or apart in the course of gameplay by the regulatory machinations of Columbia's tyrannical land and labor barons, Zachary Hale Comstock and Jeremiah Fink.

The rationale for such machinations is evidenced by Comstock and Fink's treatment of individuals in Columbia who pose a threat to the city's financial practices and undergirding technologies. For example, when the game begins the player finds the most dangerous force within the city, Elizabeth Comstock, in a massive complex that, the player later learns, siphons her inter-dimensional powers. However, an even greater demonstration of Comstock and Fink's technological mastery can be seen in the sharp racial divides they manage to maintain their social and geographic manipulations. Just as Elizabeth is sapped of her radical economic potential by her special island prison, so are Columbia's African-American, Irish, and Chinese populations, who are under the boot heels of a social engineering project that has the quite literal forces of regional convergence and divergence as its underpinning.

The significance of this market to the player's experience of wealth and the wealthy can be seen in several of the game's major scenarios. A portion of *BioShock Infinite* is concerned with DeWitt's efforts to secure arms for a worker's revolution, under the banner of a group called the *Vox Populi*. In his initial efforts to locate these arms, DeWitt discovers that the arms maker has already been murdered by Fink's police force. Dewitt is then invited to continue his pursuit in another dimension, in another version of Columbia where the laborer is still alive but where, DeWitt comes to learn, the essential role of wealth in society remains unchanged, even though it is associated with a different face. DeWitt takes the plunge, and while he manages to secure the arms for the *Vox Populi*'s rebellion, the ensuing revolt is ill-fated and does not result in the people's victory over the land and labor barons. Rather, it only anticipates a series of events that result in Elizabeth's installation as the new and terrible head of Columbia's technocratic state, where she maintains and exacerbates the essential divisions that were established by Comstock and Fink. Her ascendency and its terrible consequences are realized in a portion of the game that takes place in 1984, in a remarkable scene during which Elizabeth leverages Columbia's technological superiority to destroy New York City, and presumably other large financial centers.

From these scenarios and developments, it is reasonable to conclude that Columbia's social significance is determined by its unique technologies, which delimit the city in the sky's economic conditions, and the possibilities its citizens have for determining their cultural relevance within the context of the city itself. The power of such determination is underscored in the game's zero-sum conclusion, when DeWitt comes to learn that his very sense of self—as, importantly, an individual of few to modest means in society—has also been determined by the Lutece technology. DeWitt learns that he is an earlier version of Comstock taken from another dimension in which DeWitt has not yet embarked on the technological rebellion that led to his creation of the cult that would ascend to Columbia. The revelation has significance to the game's commentary on the association of the lower and upper classes in society, insofar as it indicates that the evident distinctions between these classes are both formulated and regulated by a surreal and mysterious determining technology—in this case the Lutece technology—that made the city and its interdimensional-traveling citizens possible, for reasons that are surreal and mysterious in the end.

The relevance of these themes and concerns to Piketty's markets is startling. However, what is not yet clear is whether, and to what extent, these themes may be descriptive of a player's act of play: for example, of a specific fantasy that rationalizes the experience of play. To determine whether such fantasy can be associated with gameplay, generally, and to *BioShock Infinite*, specifically, the work must turn to an extended consideration of the history and development of videogame narratives. That investigation constitutes a significant portion of this book, and is used to frame arguments bearing on several titles. Insofar as *BioShock Infinite* dramatizes a fanciful relationship between social classes and technology to the end of underscoring the surreal and mysterious impact technology can have on people, it speaks to an expansive catalogue of games that approach the same concern from various perspectives. An identification, analysis, and alignment of these titles illustrates shifting economic perceptions from the millennial period with significance to Piketty's statistical modeling and basic claims about the Western imagination. This work will be divided into six chapters.

Chapter 2, "Literary Theory for Gamers," introduces and aligns the three major theoretical perspectives that inform the argument. These perspectives are derived from Thomas Piketty, Joan Shelley Rubin, and Northrop Frye. The work begins with a celebration of Piketty's recent findings, but also a condemnation of his general comments on narrative structures and their significance to national notions of wealth. Rubin is then introduced as a conceptual alternative for some of the more troubling notions in Piketty, and, finally, Frye is introduced and associated with the relevant theories to the end of crafting an analytical framework for associating Piketty's economic concerns with literary subjects. From this position, the chapter notes recent work that has successfully employed Frye to address economic concerns in select videogames from the turn of the century, and the chapter advances the notion that such and similar subjects are ripe for further analysis. This notion is founded on a consideration of the unique form and function of videogames, which offer, as Alexander Galloway and Edward Castronova explain, the unique experience of action in the service of a modeled system. This distinctive dimension of the videogame form enables the player to act within the confines of a realist or fantastic economic system, and thus has the potential to comment on real-world economic conditions. The chapter ends by noting that the anticipated argument will illustrate how a number of titles do exactly this and have special relevance to Piketty's economic scheme. An exploration of these subjects provides new insight into the history of videogame narratives. The chapter concludes by demonstrating the proposed analysis with a consideration of what is generally identified as the first videogame, *Spacewar!*.

Chapter 3, "The Symbolic Order of Action and Possibility Bearing on Time," addresses the prime roles of represented wealth in videogames from the twentieth century. Providing a rationale for the application of Northrup Frye and Gérard Genette's literary theories to non-prose subjects, the argument explores the significance of capital exchange as a theme in titles such as *Spacewar!, The Oregon Trail, Pac Man,* and *Super Mario Brothers.* These titles contribute to the tradition of sentimental romance with imaginative schemes for representing and valuing player action as it bears on the player's time of play. "The Symbolic Order of Action and Possibility Bearing on Time" concludes with an exploration of such orders as they exist beyond the immediate gaming experience—that is, in the fictions of "lore" that are often generated around represented capital in videogames.

Chapter 4, "Capital and Class Determinations in Videogames," addresses theories of narrative in videogame scholarship. Focusing on observations from Alexander Galloway, Edward Castronova, and David M. Leeson, the argument attends to scholarly considerations of narrative that fail to define the term. Asserting that Genette's definition for narrative is essentially compatible with much of what is best in such criticism, the chapter establishes a related argument on the significance of capital and class determinations in videogame narratives from the first decade of the twenty-first century. The argument concludes with an assertion that *Halo: Combat Evolved* (2001) and *World of Warcraft* (2004) illuminate the prime symbolic orders of action and possibility bearing on time that shaped the player's act of play during the millennial period.

Chapter 5, "Night World Identity Affirmations," considers gamer identity and its relationship to representations of wealth in videogames. Drawing from McKenzie Wark, Ian Bogost, and Nick Dyer-Witheford and Grieg de Peuter, the argument posits that Frye's conception of the hero in the underworld has special bearing on the player's act of play in titles from the period of the Global Great Recession. Highlighting the significance of surreal and mysterious wealth in such tales to the final affirmation of the hero's identity, the chapter examines the relevance of player inventory systems to the concluding moments of *BioShock* and *Mass Effect*—both of which underscore the illusion of player choice at the same moment they affirm the hero's individuality.

Chapter 6, "Conclusion: The Wealth of Virtual Nations," affirms the limitations of the proposed program and outlines paths for future inquiry in subsequent considerations of wealth and capital in videogame narratives. Special attention is paid to the speculative applications of Genette's major theories to the videogame form as well as individual videogames. This work anticipates extended considerations of Frye's general literary theories and their bearing on videogames—as well as specific considerations of the ways in which economic aspirations and anxieties can be associated with videogames from select periods and nations.

CHAPTER 2

Literary Theory for Gamers

Abstract Crowley presents a rationale for investigating videogames as literature. Attending to Thomas Piketty's arguments on the roles of wealth in literature, Crowley draws attention to an intersection of Piketty's claims with literary critic Northrup Frye's commentary on fairy tales and sentimental romance. As well as addressing a rationale for valuing videogames as literature, Crowley posits that the videogame form itself has special meaning for what Frye identifies as fundamental themes in sentimental romance: the themes of ascent and descent. "Literary Theory for Gamers" concludes with an application of the chapter's central propositions to one of the earliest videogames, *Spacewar!*.

Keywords Thomas Piketty · Joan Shelley Rubin · Northrop Frye · Sentimental romance · Spacewar! · Videogames

In *Capital in the Twenty-First Century,* Thomas Piketty argues that financial markets can and do influence how readers imagine wealth and the wealthy in prose fiction.[1] It is a fascinating claim that rests on a debatable correlation between the act of writing about wealth and the act of reading about wealth. However, and despite this correlation, the notion is quite useful for understanding conspicuous wealth and its various representations in emerging media in the nineteenth and twentieth centuries—particularly within American markets. It establishes a general rationale for

© The Author(s) 2017
A. Crowley, *The Wealth of Virtual Nations,*
DOI 10.1007/978-3-319-53246-2_2

valuing wealth representations in narrative structures and has special relevance to entertainments from the digital age, such as those that are facilitated by the videogame form as it is understood by critics like Alexander Galloway and Edward Castronova. While Piketty does not address the videogame form itself, his arguments can be refined and made productive for such analysis with contextualizing arguments from Joan Shelley Rubin on the relationship between transatlantic gentility and emerging media, and from Northrop Frye on the transhistorical capacities of sentimental romance to represent ascendant aspirations and anxieties within cultures undergoing dramatic transformations. Collectively, a triangulation of these arguments establishes a path for considering how the videogame form may engage the social reality of the player, as well as how the modern player has been primed by larger social conditions to conceptualize his or her relationship with individual videogames.

Piketty begins with the rather conventional notion that nineteenth-century novels are "full of detailed information about the relative wealth and living standards of different social groups, and especially about the deep structure of inequality, the way it is justified, and its impact on individual lives."[2] He singles out Jane Austen and Honoré de Balzac who, among others, render what Piketty describes as "striking portraits of the distribution of wealth in Britain and France between 1790 and 1830." He then claims that they were successful in such endeavors because they were "intimately acquainted with the hierarchy of wealth in their respective societies" and somehow "grasped the hidden contours of wealth and its inevitable implications for the lives of men and women." Piketty then raises the nature and purpose of his praise by an order of magnitude with the self-deprecating admission that Austen and Balzac "depicted the effects of inequality with a verisimilitude and evocative power that no statistical or theoretical analysis can match."

It is hard to find fault with this general celebration of Austen and Balzac as well as other authors Piketty singles out in this way. However, readers should be less willing to fall into agreement with the author when he describes the much more speculative subject of national perceptions of wealth at the turn of the nineteenth century. Piketty's relevant claims extend from a central notion, repeated throughout the text, that the author's own market modeling is simply the most accurate representation of wealth distribution that has been developed to date.[3] The validity of such claims is well beyond the scope of this book, though it has garnered the attention of a number of notable scholars, such as David Campbell[4] and Eli Cook.[5] However, these same claims fall squarely within a general exploration of literature and literary audiences when Piketty references his own materialist models as primary evidence for what are generally claims about aesthetic value.

This tendency is most evident in his comments on national conceptions of wealth bearing on literature at the turn of the nineteenth century in England and France, and in early twentieth-century America. For example, speaking of France at the beginning of the nineteenth century, Piketty writes, "Contemporary readers were well aware that it took capital on the order of 1 million francs to produce an annual rent of 50,000 francs. For nineteenth-century novelists and their readers, the relation between capital and annual rent was self-evident."[6] The claim that market stability can or should compel a "self-evident" national conception of wealth—even within the particular confines of select readerships—is not above suspicion. For example, what does it mean for people to share a "self-evident" view of anything, to say nothing of something as prone to engendering febrile emotions as wealth? Without attending to such matters, Piketty simply charges ahead, noting that Austen and Balzac "frequently described the income and wealth of their characters in francs or pounds...because these quantities established a character's social status in the mind of the reader. Everyone knew what standard of living these numbers represented."[7] Using his own models as evidence, he argues that this knowledge was common in "the eighteenth century because it was a period during which per capita grew very slowly. In Great Britain, the average income was on the order of 30 pounds a year in the early 1800s, when Jane Austen wrote her novels." However, by Piketty's own logic, the people of the eighteenth century simply could not have known enough to have known what they are purported to "have known"—and this is because Piketty's data is relevant to his own, supposedly cutting-edge, twenty-first-century modeling. All of this is not to say that such populations could not have conceptualized wealth in ways that mirror Piketty's findings, but the paradox can draw attention to the fact that Piketty is making assumptions in the service of his own findings and conclusions.

Such reasoning is part of a larger, equally assumptive commentary on the supposed role of wealth in "literature" in Western markets. In one of the more perplexing logical moves in the text, Piketty sets his supposedly economically aligned, eighteenth-century readerships up as a counterpoint to post-Great War readers in the twentieth century. He notes, "Until

World War I, money had meaning, and novelists did not fail to exploit it, explore it, and turn it into a literary subject."[8] He then goes on to claim, "Specific references to wealth and income were omnipresent in the literature of all countries before 1914; these references gradually dropped out of sight between 1914 and 1945 and never truly reemerged."[9] This observation—validated nowhere in the text—is peculiar for at least two reasons. Setting aside for a moment the God-like perspective it seems to convey regarding the author's knowledge of "literature," it also seems to imply that "references to wealth" are and should be understood as specific, numerated references to national currency. Even if one allows for the possibility that there is—in some imaginary tally of global "literature"—a marked decline in such numbers, this would not prove Piketty's larger comment about references to wealth, which surely had as many possible artistic representations prior to the Great War as after the Great War.

While these sorts of fallacies challenge a reading of *Capital in the Twenty-First Century*, they do not necessarily undermine the text: rather, they are better understood as evidence of what is by many accounts a staggeringly successful materialist program struggling to articulate its own broader social significance. To date, the general question of whether the document has social significance appears to have been settled by the many and varied scholars and critics, hailing from numerous fields, who have embraced the work and its findings. However, in terms of literary studies, the question of whether *Capital in the Twenty-First Century* has the kind of significance the author appears to desire is certainly an open question.

Nevertheless, and despite these concerns, there is evidence in the text indicating that Piketty is capable of a nuanced understanding of the role of wealth in literature and literary societies. This becomes apparent when the author begins to discuss the concept of narrative structure. He writes, "In most of these novels, the financial, social, and psychological setting is established in the first few pages and occasionally alluded to thereafter, so that the reader will not forget everything that sets the characters of the novel apart from the rest of society: the monetary markers that shape their lives, their rivalries, their strategies, and their hopes."[10] The notion that these "markers" are presented with attendant psychological details is particularly intriguing, especially in light of Piketty's comments about the shared conceptions of wealth that supposedly defined Austen and Balzac's readerships. For example, should readers assume that these audiences would have similarly shared understandings of these multifaceted and overdetermined aspects of the human experience? Surely not, and there is good evidence in the text indicating that Piketty would agree that such understanding would not be shared. For example, he notes that select nineteenth-century authors approach the concept of wealth in society from a deeply subjective position: for example, they are "obsessed" with it. He writes, "If inherited wealth is omnipresent in nineteenth-century novels, it was not only because writers, especially the debt-ridden Balzac, were obsessed by it. It was above all because inheritance occupied a structurally central place in nineteenth-century society—central as both economic flow and social force."[11] While he celebrates Balzac's financial perspective elsewhere, the notion of obsessed authors composing literary representations of wealth underscores the subjectivity of such narration, both for the realization of wealth in narrative and for the reception of such realizations in the reading public.

To his credit, Piketty edges ever closer to a formal consideration of such questions and to possible points of departure for considering select novels in actual detail. He notes, for example, that while numeric references to wealth in the form of currency are significant, there are "many other forms of capital, some of them quite 'dynamic,' that play a role in the identified novels."[12] Such forms of wealth emerge around what he identifies as "archetypes." He writes, "Indeed, the characters in nineteenth-century novels often seem like archetypes of the rentier, a suspect figure in the modern era of democracy and meritocracy."[13] These observations lead to questions about not only the nature, value, and use of various sources and kinds of wealth in the identified novels, but also about their association with the identified archetype, to say nothing about the general questions that could then be asked about such archetypes in literature. These concerns suggest that Piketty's criticism of literature has analytical potentials that exceed his base position regarding reader sameness.

Of course, these objections connote no resistance on my part to Piketty's larger points regarding the general financial stability of select European markets at the beginning of the nineteenth century. However, they should give pause to the notion that such markets are totalizing contextual frames for rationalizing the utility of wealth representations in the identified works. Yet, at the same time, it is perfectly reasonable to ask whether the practical economic pressures undergirding these models are significant to the identified narratives. To that concern, Piketty offers little to facilitate actual analysis, as his literary investigations are generally truncated plot summaries in support of anecdotal developments, offered without a broader academic or aesthetic perspective.

The critical limitations of his approach become quite apparent when Piketty tries to expand his commentary to consider works from non-European cultures. For example, he notes, "The novels of Henry James that are set in Boston and New York between 1880 and 1910 also show social groups in which real estate and industrial and financial capital matter almost as much as in European novels: times had indeed changed since the Revolutionary War, when the United States was still a land without capital."[14] The literary claim stands squarely on Piketty's economic modeling, which may be a bellwether work of statistical analysis, but is problematic to the extent that, in this instance, it conveys a supposed one-to-one correlation between European markets from the turn of the nineteenth century and North American markets at the turn of the twentieth. This problem rises from more than a notion that these markets would have similar social concerns supporting their seemingly now-aligned capital conditions—which were an entire ocean and century away from each other. It also reminds us, or should remind us, that the identified authors stand on rich artistic traditions, traditions that may intersect but which are often divergent in their proportions, a fact that was surely as true of Austen and Balzac as it is of Austen, Balzac, and James.

Yet, as *Capital in the Twenty-First Century* underscores the significance of national markets to literature, and as Piketty's modeling does by all accounts confront modern readers with a stunningly specific exploration of wealth inequality, it is reasonable to ask how this new model may be productive for established arguments on the history of artistic representations of wealth in literature. This is particularly relevant to contemporary audiences and media, given Piketty's dire observation that contemporary life occurs in the context of such divergent levels of wealth in society that modern poor and middle-class individuals have essentially lost the ability to conceptualize wealth, and by extension recognize or represent it in life and literature. He writes,

> For this half of the population, the very notions of wealth and capital are relatively abstract. For millions of people, "wealth" amounts to little more than a few weeks' wages in a checking account or low-interest savings account, a car, and a few pieces of furniture. The inescapable reality is this: wealth is so concentrated that a large segment of society is virtually unaware of its existence, so that some people imagine that it belongs to surreal or mysterious entities. That is why it is so essential to study capital and its distribution in a methodical, systematic way.[15]

In terms of the American experience—and the actual social concerns that have long been associated with the works of Henry James and similar authors from the end of the nineteenth century—a consideration of how representations of wealth contribute to national notions of capital could begin with a consideration of Joan Shelley Rubin's *The Making of Middlebrow Culture*.

The Making of Middlebrow Culture is one of several noteworthy end-of-the-millennium texts concerned with the history of culture and class in the USA. Rubin's essential argument stands on the notion that the so-called genteel tradition did not, as others have argued, conclude with the Great War, but, rather, persisted into the twentieth century.[16] Her arguments extend from the position that American conceptions of gentility—long regarded as historical artifacts of the nineteenth century—have strong and unexamined roots in the eighteenth century. From this position, she explores the relevance of such concerns to a range of media that emerged at the beginning of the twentieth century and considers how these media were used to drive market interest in narratives concerned with wealth. In its totality, Rubin's commentary stands as a productive context for Piketty's models of wealth in the early American experience, as it addresses the social conditions that likely bore on American readers of not only Austen and Balzac, but also on American authors like James, who also wrote with the "invisible contours of wealth" in mind.[17]

American conceptions of gentility, Rubin explains, were forged in the early eighteenth century "by the gentry who...populated the 'great houses' of the Eastern seaboard."[18] They "combined the British legacy of insistence on fine manners, proper speech, and elegance with the demand, in the American setting, for moral substance." In its early formulations, this combination of ideals resulted in a materialist view of gentility, a "high style" perpetuated by a cultural elite, defined by "parlor furnishings, rare wines, fine china—and books—that bespoke their sense of propriety and grace."[19] While the tendency to "associate genuine cultivation" and inward virtue...with materialism deepened and spread" after 1800, the uniquely American drive toward a democratization of "property ownership and the rise of republicanism enhanced the prospect that Americans of more modest means could attain the respectability formerly limited to the aristocracy."[20] This transformation had literary consequences for the new republic, primarily in the form of "popular advice manuals," which stressed the notion that "genteel conduct did not depend on financial resources."[21] In terms of Piketty's comments on national conceptions of wealth, the financial and social turbulence indicated by such manuals would seem to belie the notion that wealth—stable or otherwise—is necessarily regarded within complex populations as a "given." Rather, from the position of the poor, the more imperative concern could be summarized with the question of how individuals acquire it, given their social positioning.

For Rubin, demonstrable evidence of these shifting values can be found in the explosion of American institutions that were taken with such interests in the nineteenth century. Americans of modest means were deeply involved in considering aesthetic conceptions of "character," "fineness," "taste," "culture," and "personality" through the organs of the library system, American publishing houses, higher education, and the lecture circuit—all of which opened innumerable new pathways for voices who wished to contribute to explorations of and elaborations upon "the best" kinds of refinements, including literary refinements. It is no surprise, then, as Rubin points out, that in the second half of the nineteenth century so many Americans were primed to celebrate the writing of Matthew Arnold. In terms of Piketty's argument, the American celebration of Arnold is exceptionally relevant to Henry James, who wrote, "I shall not go so far as to say of Mr. Arnold that he invented [culture], but he made it more definite than it had been before—he vivified and lighted it up."[22] Such lightening, for James, extends from the Arnoldian focus on "the best that has been thought and said in the world" over the best that might be purchase or otherwise acquired in the world through commerce. In this context, it is reasonable for Piketty to notice that James attends to different forms of wealth than the forms that were most relevant to the American economy after the revolution. However, Piketty's commentary implies that this transformation has a direct market explanation and does not attend to the broader social and philosophical trends bearing on gentility that were surely relevant to such markets, and which render pure financial valuations of capital suspect. While such trends are not central to Piketty's argument, the fact that he writes as if he were considering them—though without any evident support—is noteworthy and bears consideration.

Nevertheless, a combination of Rubin and Piketty can lead to productive questions about how authors like James might realize the markets of their day in ways that speak to shifting American conceptions of gentility adapting Arnoldian social "standards" to everyday life. This is, as Rubin explains, the relevant context of what George Santayana coins the "genteel tradition" in 1911.[23] At the moment of Santayana's postulation—and in ways that are consistent with Piketty's modeling—the Western world was already starting to buckle under the consequences of increased industrialization, which would become inescapable during the Great War. For some, Rubin notes, this transformation was already sounding the death knell for America's traditional conceptions of the well-to-do. However, she contends that, while several critics see that period as the natural conclusion for such nineteenth-century aspirations, the largely European conflict did not undermine the primary social assumptions behind American conceptions of gentility—particularly (and ironically, perhaps) in terms of its bearing on consumerism. This is because the Arnoldian position does not simply hold that the individual should advance certain standards as sacred to personal development and integrity. It also advocates for the equally important notion that the wrong kinds of cultural experiences—and the wrong kinds of books—are harmful to the individual. For Rubin, the notions that there are informative and damaging works of art and that the consumer must carefully navigate between such items are the compelling concerns of the genteel tradition in the Post-War Period. She then contends that the media that emerged during this period —for example, radio, film, and later television—would essentially become the Post-War battlefields for articulating American conceptions of gentility —the new arenas within which marketers and cultural demagogues would broadcast increasingly divergent notions of gentility-through-consumption to their respective audiences.

For Rubin, these and related battles have had a profound impact on life in the late twentieth century and millennial period. She writes,

> [W]hile the market remains capable of disseminating the importance of reading...its capacity to subvert genuine understanding and autonomy survives and flourishes as well. The stakes in what H. G. Wells called the "race between education and catastrophe" currently seem higher than ever. While recognizing the drawbacks and limitations of the middlebrow perspective, one might thus hope to recover the moral and aesthetic commitments which the makers of middlebrow culture at their best tried to diffuse.[24]

Such diffusion has strong associations with notions of wealth, as well as with representations of wealth in American culture, literary or otherwise. In this way, Rubin's comments on the race between education and catastrophe have bearing on Piketty's comments on the modern market's impact on the average person's ability to conceptualize wealth.

However, while Rubin's argument provides social structuring for Piketty's literary analysis, it is also the case that her argument is exceedingly general in its narrative evaluations. Often, Rubin simply gestures towards kinds of literature while reasoning, or makes broad generalizations about the collected works of individual authors in support of her social theories. Consequently, before it will be possible to ascertain what either commentator's perspective can bring to a literary investigation, these perspectives must first be aligned with a unifying theory of narrative. Given the historical, social, and limited literary interests in *Capital in the Twenty-First Century* and *The Making of Middlebrow Culture*, these works can be united with Northrop Frye's general theories on literature from the nineteenth and twentieth centuries in *The Secular Scripture: A Study of the Structure of Romance*. A foundation for such association is Frye's shared interests in representations of wealth in nineteenth- and twentieth-century literature—particularly in the writing of Austen, Balzac, and James—as well as his interest in class-based evaluations of popular literatures in Western readerships.

Frye identifies the romance as a longstanding and remarkably stable literary genre. His argument extends from several assumptions and terms that bear review. For Frye, the romance and indeed all prose fiction emerges from a "middle earth" that can be adjudicated in terms of its similarity with the reader's own world of lived experience.[25] If this space is defined with anti-representational people, places, things, and a plot or plots determined by coincidence, it is said to be "romantic." However, should the operative middle earth correlate with lived experience, it is "realistic." For Frye, realist fiction is perhaps no more than a historical anomaly, with roots in the advent and early developmental period of the novel. The sentimental romance, on the other hand, has deep roots extending to the late classical period—and fruit-laden branches in contemporary society.[26]

Frye identifies several key characteristics of the romance. He notes its tendency to begin with a "sharp descent in social status, from riches to poverty from privilege to slavery,"[27] and then to develop in the hero or heroine's pursuit of love, through a series of discontinuous episodes concerning events involving—but not limited to—"mysterious births, oracular prophecies about the future contortions of the plot,...adventures that involve pirates, narrow escapes from death" and the like.[28] Such works stand in the service of the "imaginative needs of [their] community,"[29] and can be divided into basic categories. These divisions stand on another fundamental assumption, which is that the content of any given romance can be broken down into "units."[30] These units are defined by the trans-historical images that are conveyed by the narrative. For Frye, such images stand as a kind of "metaphor." Frye uses the term to denote the relational significance of the image to other images in the romance, and not—as one might with a more traditional use of the term—to some subject that exists beyond the context of the romantic tradition. His logic stands on the notion that the longevity of the romance as a genre has been facilitated by the multicultural relevance of select or similar images across time. General details associated with select images may change between distinct iterations of the romance, but these changes, Frye notes, rarely disrupt the funda-mental value of the image and its associated images.

With this scheme, he claims that most societies produce two romantic traditions: one in which the fundamental images are recast with divine or otherwise culturally sacrosanct subjects that imbue the romance with cultural authority, and also those that draw the fundamental images with secular subjects with limited cultural relevance, and which are germane to the narrative's period of production. He identifies the former category as the "mythical" mode and the latter as the "fabulous" mode.[31] While certainly grand and contestable, this theory and its categorical divisions holds special relevance for Piketty and Rubin's arguments. It allows for the possibility that financial and related genteel concerns in literature might be as relevant to specific literary conventions as they might be to national socioeconomic developments. Frye also provides a scheme for adjudicat-ing the significance of such concerns within the context of a single narrative.

According to Frye, the middle earth that underlies the romance as well as more contemporary notions of fiction always exists in the context of three other "worlds," which he organizes into a basic hierarchy. He writes, "The highest level is heaven.... [The next] is earthly paradise, where man lived before the fall.... [The third] is the world of ordinary experience we now live in."[32] This third-order world is the middle earth that unites realist and romantic work, and which tends to be the sole concern in realist works. Below the middle earth, there is a fourth world, a demonic world or hell, usually placed below ground. In the context of these various worlds, Frye argues that there are essentially four basic moves in literature, and individual images and their associated relationships with other images can be valued against their contributions to such movements. There is the descent from a higher world; the descent to a lower world; the ascent from a lower world; and an ascent to a higher world. While these paired movements may sound redundant, the key notion here is in the focus of the narrative. For example, the descent from a higher world and the descent to a lower world would be distinguished by the former's attention to a higher world and the latter's attention to a lower world and would come with a distinct set of unit associations that are particular to such movement.

In this context, it is possible to determine that Piketty and Rubin value authors like Austen, Balzac, and James for their representations of financial concerns that affirm key realist market- and class-based assumptions: for example, in ways that are significant to discrete cultures at the moment of their composition. Before addressing the larger question of whether or not these representations are in some sense accurate to lived experience, it would be reasonable to consider the extent to which the world of experience in these texts is in and of itself realistic or romantic, and on what or which narrative levels such realism or romance might be more or less relevant to the involved worlds, and also how these varying levels might contribute to the metaphorical implications of the narrative's aligned units. For example, Frye considers Austen, Balzac, and James, and is quick to note that their writing is far from realistic, as their plots depend on impossible coincidences and the unrealistic unions of people who—in the world of lived experience—could not be expected to marry.[33] He explicitly associates Austen, Balzac, James and others with a creative interest in uniting the coincidental storytelling tendencies of the romance with the supposedly realist concerns of the novel. From this, it can be concluded that, regardless of their apparent verisimilitude, the markets referenced in such texts are potentially fabulous conventions inserted into age-old romantic structures with literary significance that exceeds their presumed economic acuity.

While this commentary could begin with considerations of Austen, Balzac, and James, it is important to note that Piketty and Rubin's essential relevance to Frye does not actually extend from their arguments on these authors. Rather, their significance extends from a general insistence that narrative structure is relevant to and affirms their individual arguments, which concern pragmatic realities of lived experience that have significance to what can be dubbed the middle earths in select narratives. Frye's conception of ascent and descent in relation to middle earth indicates a matrix of structural possibilities with fundamental interpretive

2 LITERARY THEORY FOR GAMERS 33

values that bring meaning to, rather than derive meaning from, Pikettian and Rubinian concepts. The broad critical possibilities of an alignment between Frye, Piketty, and Rubin are hinted at in recent work by David M. Leeson, which attends to elements in romantic structures in videogame narratives.

Leeson makes the interesting observation that the so-called "single-player shooter" videogame genre, which emerged in the early 1990s, affirms many of the structural concerns discussed in *The Secular Scripture*. Leeson selects this genre for consideration based on its popularity and the observation that single-player shooters can be distinguished from multiplayer shooters under the notion that single-player shooters are "story-driven" while multiplayer shooters are supposedly "gameplay-driven."[34] The argument is largely associative, with Leeson drawing from various comments Frye makes about the theme of descent, primarily from middle earth to an underworld or hellscape: that is, the descent to a lower world. As part of this gloss on assumed single-player shooter story structure, he makes an interesting connection between the theme of descent in the romance and the tendency for "shooter" videogames to begin with what Frye describes as "a sharp descent in social status, from riches to poverty, from privilege to a struggle to survive, or even slavery."[35] It is an interesting observation that Leeson does not explore in detail. This is not necessarily a weakness in the argument, which is concerned with a novel-enough-in-its-own-context broad stroke association between Frye's description of the romance and digital storytelling. Nevertheless, given that Frye is quite explicit about the relevance of the realistic or romantic qualities of middle earth to the process of ascent or descent, Leeson's comments raise questions about how, why, and to what extent the movement towards poverty and the hellscape are related under modern conceptions of capital, to the extent that such conceptions are present in the videogame.

While the pursuit of such connections would be intriguing, it would also overlook the larger implication of Leeson's argument, which is simply that there is a meaningful association to be made between the realization of poverty in videogame narratives and Frye's conception of the romance. For instance, what might emerge from a structural consideration not only of "shooter" games but also the general history of videogames, from their origins in the late 1940s to the present period? Are there pathways within the medium for productive considerations of discrete or collective titles as romantic subjects—or if not as romantic subjects *per se*, then as subjects with significance to the romance and its conceptualization in the latter half of the twentieth century and millennial period? These questions become even more intriguing considering Piketty's findings. Piketty's financial modeling stands as a potentially excellent resource for determining the market relevance of wealth representations in individual titles, to ascertain whether they contribute to a given middle earth's realism or romanticism during its period of composition and initial distribution. Moreover, and in similar ways, Rubin's social history of the cultural values of wealth representations in America provides a parallel perspective for adjudicating the utility of wealth representations in specific titles, to the end of determining whether they speak to the potentially fabulous concerns of an era or to the mythological roles of wealth in America. The proposed critical triangulation has the potential to expand upon the involved perspectives in ways that contribute to emerging discussions on the structure of videogame narratives.

The promise of the analytical scheme extends from the notion that Frye's view of the romance can be reconciled with gaming structures. The possibility is not alien to Frye, and he identifies one commonality between these subjects early in his argument. He writes,

> In the general area of romance, we find highly stylized patterns like the detective story, which are so conventionalized as to resemble games. We expect each game of chess to be different, but we do not want the conventions of the game itself to alter, or to see a chess game in which the bishops move in straight lines and the rooks diagonally.[36]

It is an interesting association. However, as Frye never returns to this notion it is reasonable to wonder how or if the relationship might be expressed in terms of his comments on middle earth, unit, and metaphor. For example, if as Frye contends some notion of middle earth is fundamental to the romance, it would be interesting to consider if a similar concept could be associated with chess. Insofar as middle earth is essentially defined as a plane of causality, within which the orderly progression of distinct units is informative of an organizing structure, the concept seems compatible with the experience of chess. The linkage becomes more significant under the notion that, for Frye, romantic units are bound by their interdependent metaphorical significance: that is, each image finds larger meaning in its association with antecedent and subsequent images, which also derive meaning from their own antecedent and subsequent images—the totality of which expresses the logic of romance. In chess, the pieces and their positions can also be conceived of as unit images, images that derive meaning from their adhesion to a formal structure, one that dictates the relevance of any unit development at any point in the game in terms associated with the history of that specific game as well as with its potential future.

However, it is also the case that this same reasoning reveals the limitation of any association of chess and the romance over the concept of middle earth. The nature of this limitation is indicated in Frye's comment regarding what it is that the reader of romance and the player of chess "do not want." For Frye, the romance is evidence of humankind's efforts to create a kind of order and meaning in the face of the chaos of actual experience. This order bears on matters of the heart, which are pursued but rarely reconciled in lived experience, but which tend to find resolution and affirmation in the romance.[37] For Frye, divergent cultures will address the romantic structure with distinct totems, values, and cultural practices for calling such enterprises into the service of everyday experience—to make it accessible to the imaginative needs of the moment. While it is similarly true that chess provides the illusion of order to the effect of imbuing time with socially-determined value—it is also true that the goal of chess is, frankly, chess. If the human heart gets involved, it does so at its own peril. For this reason, an analysis of chess as chess that adheres to the essential values of the romance, or vice versa will lead the critic into strange and sterile territory.

Moreover, it should be noted that even when a game stands intentionally in reference to the romantic tradition, that alone is not enough to justify a romantic reading of the subject. This point can be illuminated with a consideration of what is generally regarded as the first significant computer-based game with a graphical interface: *Spacewar!*. *Spacewar!* emerged at the beginning of the 1960s, during a moment when, according to Frye, the romance had a newly acquired "lease on fashion" with "the success and the rise of what is generally called science fiction," which—for Frye—began in the mid-1950s.[38] Frye explains that in "science fiction the characters may be earthlings, the setting the intergalactic spaces, and what gets wrecked in hostile territory a spaceship, but the tactics of the storyteller generally conform to much the same outlines."[39] The rise of science fiction was relevant to the creators of *Spacewar!*, who derived their concept from the Buck Rogers novels, as well as other "trashy sci-fi books," such as those in the *Lensman* and *Skylark* series—works that are full of interplanetary and interstellar travel, with all the predictable conflicts, crashes, and intrigue long associated with much more earthly seafaring tales.[40]

In terms of Frye's fundamental concepts, *Spacewar!*'s "middle earth" has unit elements with relevance to the tradition of the fabulous—or inventive—romance. As Frye indicates with a quote from Jorges Luis Borges, the image of a ship adrift is the defining image of the fabulous romance, which Borges sets in opposition to romance in the mythic mode, which he defines with the image of Deicide.[41] Notably, the drifting ships in *Spacewar!* are non-representational, which is another key feature of fabulous romance. Though they are based in the technology of that era, the weaponized interstellar battle vehicles in the game have no corollary in the actual world. Consequently, the scenario depicted in *Spacewar!* contains a gesture to fabulous romance. Such romance, Frye explains, derives its material "from traditions [that] may have no recognized or understood social status."[42] This status can be correlated with the status of science fiction sources that were relevant to the game's composition. The cultural authority of such writing at the time, from a genteel perspective and many others was extremely limited and stands as further evidence that *Spacewar!* can be associated with the fabulous tradition of sentimental romance.

However, while *Spacewar!* contains a strong association with sentimental romance in the fabulous mode at the level of scenario, it does not contain the kinds of progressive unit associations that undergird Frye's conception of narrative development in actual examples of the romance, either in their truncated—for example, fairy tale or otherwise "naive" manifestations—or in their extended prose-based formulations.[43] For example, the experience of gameplay does not correlate with the general themes of ascent or descent that are fundamental to the genre. This is not the same as saying that the game lacks a narrative, as there is clearly action over time with consequences in *Spacewar!*. However, that action does not allow for the alignment of discontinuous, anti-representational occurrences into the historical shape and related purposes of sentimental romance.

With Leeson's argument in mind, *Spacewar!* and the essentially similar titles that followed it into the world indicate that there is an artistic gesture towards the fabulous romance in the advent of the videogame. The question of how this gesture may have developed over time into, as Leeson notes, the adoption of complete romantic structures by the mid- to late-1990s is intriguing for a range of reasons—though it is perhaps not very surprising, given Frye's comments on just how invasive the romance has been across various media for millennia. Indeed, it is precisely for this reason that the general question of whether there are videogames that adhere to romantic conventions is less compelling than the question of whether it is possible to identify examples of romantic videogame narratives that—through their distinctive or otherwise fabulous features—speak to imaginative needs bearing on transitory notions of wealth and social positioning. The purpose of an investigation into such matters would not necessarily be to identify a chronological progression of narrative techniques. Rather, the purpose would extend from the notion that discrete works from the last half-century may be indicative of whether there is anything particular to the medium of videogames that brings meaning to or derives meaning from the structure of romance. While this is an open-ended concern, Piketty's financial modeling and Rubin's persuasive social theories underscore related notions that compel investigation. If, for example, the era of videogames is, as Piketty indicates, one in which audiences long-associated with romantic entertainment have either lost or are losing their ability to conceptualize wealth and, as Rubin explains, these same populations are drifting away from binding notions of morality and aesthetic commitment,[44] it would be important to know if videogames in the fabulous mode are engaged with these conditions to the possible benefit or detriment of players and society.

CHAPTER 3

The Symbolic Order of Action and Possibility Bearing on Time

Abstract Crowley addresses the prime roles of represented wealth in videogames from the twentieth century. Providing a rationale for the application of Northrup Frye and Gérard Genette's literary theories to non-prose subjects, Crowley explores the significance of capital exchange as a theme in titles such as *Spacewar!*, *The Oregon Trail*, *Pac Man*, and *Super Mario Brothers*. These titles contribute to the tradition of sentimental romance with imaginative schemes for representing and valuing player action as it bears on the player's time of play. "The Symbolic Order of Action and Possibility Bearing on Time" concludes with an exploration of such orders as they exist beyond the immediate gaming experience—that is, in the fictions of lore that are often generated around represented capital in videogames.

Keywords Northrop Frye · Gérard Genette · *Pac Man* · *Super Mario Brothers* · Benedict Anderson · Lore

While *Spacewar!* presents images with relevance to the sentimental romance, it is reasonable to ask whether such images warrant an association with Frye's general theories. This is because Frye's argument is bound by certain—though broad—assumptions about prose subjects and *Spacewar!* is not a prose subject. Consequently, before an analysis of *Spacewar!* or other digital entertainments can engage Frye's claims,

© The Author(s) 2017
A. Crowley, *The Wealth of Virtual Nations*,
DOI 10.1007/978-3-319-53246-2_3

significant matters of media and mode must be addressed. This work can begin with the recognition that, for Frye, romantic subjects are determined by their associated "narratives," which he considers as "verbal structures."[1] He explains that verbal structures in the genre of sentimental romance have significant—that is, definitive—grammatical investment in predictable subjects that are drawn together in the service of realizing experiences of "love and adventure."[2] From this, it can be inferred that an application of Frye's theories to a given text would at a minimum need to stand on the notion that the text conveys a verbal structure that meets these admittedly broad conditions. Fortunately, it is possible to arrive at such a determination for *Spacewar!*, and the essential logic for this determination can justify the application of Frye's theories to all the videogames under consideration in this project.

The rationale turns on the observation that Frye uses the term "verbal" to convey the concept of linguistic syntax. "Verbal" as such stands in grand reference to words and their associations. However, "verbal" has a secondary meaning that is specific to verbs themselves. Importantly—and obviously—as a category of word this secondary meaning is accounted for and compatible with the primary meaning of the word. This observation can be paired with the knowledge that at roughly the same time that Frye was formalizing his argument on romance Gérard Genette was composing his own formal definition for narrative. Genette arrives at the notion that narratives should be understood as "the expansion of a verb"[3] and argues that such expansions should be assessed under the grammar of verbs: for example, literal conceptual categories of person, tone, and mood. This proposition has led to decades of scholars and critics endeavoring to assess the relevance of verbs and verbal development in media that do not conform to the conventions of prose. The best efforts in this vein preserve the spirit of Genette's program by attending to the distinguishing features that are central to their subject's essential form: for example, styles of painting and sculpting, specific genres of film, categorical approaches in theater, and so on. In short, Genette's theories are made relevant through their rational adaptation to the medium or media at hand in such arguments. In terms of the sentimental romance, an application of Genettian terms should begin with—and sustain itself through—attention to verbal developments that occur in the service of the genre's fundamental concerns: the realization of love and adventure in verbal structures.

While this rationale may indicate a path for aligning Genette with Frye, it does not yet indicate how or why this alignment might service a consideration of videogames. Before this can happen, it would be necessary to identify an action—a verb—that is specific in its expansion to the videogame form, if only generally, and also to the realization of sentimental romance in videogames. It is the special determination of this project that the act of exchange is such an action. While I do not contend that acts of exchange are relevant to all videogames, it is possible to observe their developmental relevance to titles that draw from—or contribute to—the genre of sentimental romance. For example, *Spacewar!* makes use of exchange in ways that call to mind the basic, adventure-oriented conditions of romance. During play, there are several actions that are available to the player. She can navigate a ship and fire a blast at her opponent. However, these actions alone do not advance the gameplay scenario, other than to change the position of the player's ship, or to introduce the graphic of a blast shot across the screen. For the game to advance, such action must conclude in an exchange, with the blast hitting and destroying the enemy ship. This results in a change to the targeted ship, its destruction, and the termination of immediate play, which is then followed by the initiation of a new round. Understood broadly, such exchange can be conceptualized as exchange with the consequence of termination, and it manifests in several similar titles that would emerge at the beginning of gaming's first great wave. For example, *Space Wars* (1977), *Space Invaders* (1978), *Galaxian* (1979), and *Asteroids* (1979) all make use of exchange for termination, though it is true that the various consequences for termination and opportunities for termination range from title to title, but the essential logic holds from work to work, in terms of its bearing on a ship's relationship with another object. Importantly, and with an eye towards the project at hand, it is crucial to note that each of these games offer broader interpretive possibilities than a focused consideration of exchange for termination. Each has its own unique narrative context and slate of aesthetic concerns. Nevertheless, it is the case that they can be aligned under the offered interpretive framework, to underscore the significance of exchange for termination to games from this period.

At the same time, it is also the case that these titles can be aligned under the notion that they represent what Frye calls the "context of romance."[4] Such discourse involves a rhetorical investment in anti-representational subjects and plotting: for example, people, places, and things that do not exist or which escape a "realistic" description, which are organized under plots structures that depend heavily on coincidence, rather than practical causality. In terms of *Spacewar!* and the other identified titles, the warring space vehicles certainly fall under the category of anti-representational subjects, as they have no correlation with the known world—then or now. Moreover, the games' plots—which involve the endless manipulation and destruction of these subjects and other fantastical entities—also fall squarely within the realm of anti-representational possibility for romantic subjects in coincidental relationships.

However, while it is possible to associate these titles with the context of romance, it is also true that such association appears to be of little significance to Frye's larger theory, and this is because his argument is an assessment of literary subjects and this game fails to meet Frye's standards for such subjects. He argues that all literary subjects—romantic or otherwise—involve a character's real or symbolic movement between different symbolic or practical "worlds" of experience.[5] These worlds range from the ideal (heaven) through an earthly paradise (Eden), to the experience of pragmatic daily reality (middle earth), and finally to a night world (hell). The key notion is that the narrative ascends or descends from one location to another by either rational or irrational means into a contextually distinct scenario. In terms of *Spacewar!*, there is no evident narrative movement through or to any such worlds. Rather, the narrative unfolds in—and is essentially defined by—the same essential space, which is quite literally represented space.

Nevertheless, while these titles do not meet this standard for literary merit, they do have some bearing on the essential conditions of at least one of Frye's identified "worlds"— the "night world."[6] Frye argues that "most of what goes on in the night world of romance is cruelty and horror, yet what is essential is not cruelty as such but the presence of some kind of ritual." This ritual stands as a "vision of the absurd." In *Spacewar!*, that vision and its associated ritual plays out in the endless and essentially meaningless battle, characterized by repeated destruction facilitated by exchange for termination. This act is of equal importance to other titles from the period that resonate with Frye's conception of the night world in ways that *Spacewar!* does not. For example, Frye writes that the hero in the night world finds himself surrounded by monstrous biological forms. *Space Attack*, *Space Invaders*, and *Centipede* present experiences that fit this description, in the service of ritualized action involving anti-representational subjects engaged in coincidental relationships determined through acts of exchange.

At the same time, it should be noted that acts of exchange with out-comes other than termination are important to the development of play in a range of titles from this period. Acts of exchange for continuation and acts of exchange for failure become cornerstone concepts for players by the end of the 1970s. It is possible to isolate such acts and describe their relevance to key notions in Frye's theory. For example, in what is arguably the first videogame to represent something like a sentimental romance, *The Oregon Trail* (1974), the player engages in a number of exchange acts that facilitate the continuation of the adventure: food is exchanged for health, goods are exchanged for comfort and survival, and—perhaps most importantly in terms of the project at hand—money is exchanged for these and other items. As such, exchange in *The Oregon Trail* is distinct in kind from exchange in *Spacewar!*, where exchange arrests and re-sets play.

Ultimately, this aspect of the game is the feature that connects the title with Frye's essential conception of literature. For example, unlike *Spacewar!*, *The Oregon Trail* moves the player through distinct spaces that generally adhere to the bare essence of Frye's "pastoral" and prag-matic "middle earth" worlds. As the player moves across a world of realistic challenges, he or she comes to moments of essential respite—the well-stocked trading posts—where there are no immediate dangers, other than the challenges of commerce. While commerce is certainly not part of Frye's vision of pastoral spaces, the larger and more important point is simply that the game moves the player through the physical challenges of an inhospitable middle earth and into and out of waystations where—like the Sylvain landscape in Frye's theory of Eden—the player may find some solace from immediate challenges to life and limb. Significantly, the title's literary and romantic dimensions are extensions of its central experience of exchange for continuation, which is in large part associated with pastoral spaces with strong middle earth associations, bound by market drudgery bearing on pragmatic experience: this is the context for "adventure" in *The Oregon Trail*.

Another significant form of exchange from this period is exchange for failure. For example, in *Pong* the consequence of exchange is neither termination nor extension, but, rather, the persistence of an established state—of stasis—which persists until the act of exchange between the player and his or her opponent fails. At that moment, the game distributes points to the player who initiated the failed exchange. Thus, here as well, points—or at least the promise of points—motivates the player to execute the essential action that is necessary to advance the round and its associated narrative, no matter how thin that narrative may be. Such advancement is recorded in what amounts to the inverse of exchange dynamics in the later *Spacewar!* clones (e.g., *Galaxy Game* and *Computer Space*) that included point systems (*Spacewar!* did not): there, the point is awarded to the player who initiates the act of completed exchange. In its earliest iterations—and as evidenced by the many *Pong* clones—exchange for failure does not appear to be a relevant act in titles with weak or strong associations with the sentimental romance. However, it is nevertheless a significant feature of play during this period and crucial to the project at hand to the extent that it delimits a boundary for the project's potential applications.

However, it is the case that all three of the identified exchange acts are united under a common notion with relevance to the argument: they all bear on the distribution of points or other accrued commodities. This commonality speaks to the significance of points and the like as a determinative feature of play in these titles. Crucially, it can be observed that this relevance has unifying implications for the association of time with play. While this temporality is abstract, it is minimally indicative of the played past, present, and potential future for the player and his or her exchange acts: for example, here are points that have been acquired through means, here are the points that have been acquired at this moment through means, and here are the points the player has yet to acquire through means. The abstract, temporal context that emerges from a record of exchange indicates a symbolic order between action and possibility bearing on time. One claim in the service of this observation is that there are numerous titles from the same period in which such order emerges under other, distinct circumstances. For example, the 1970s also saw the rise of maze-based titles, such as *Space Race* (1975) and *Gran Track 10* (1975). While exchange is a feature of play in these titles, it is not manifested as an act that is determined by the player to the end of continuation, termination, or failure. Rather, exchange itself it is a determining condition of play. These titles include a literal chronological record of play—a ticking clock—the purpose of which is to determine the player's ultimate score. In this capacity, chronological time is literally a form of point keeping and stands in for the point record itself. In contrast with these titles, it can be argued that games like *Galaxy Game, The Oregon Trail,* and *Pong* affirm a point-based temporal order through exchange acts, rather than through the literal exchange of chronological time for points.

Before moving on, it should be noted that there are other titles from the period—such as *Gotcha* (1973)—that blend the temporal concerns of games like *Space Race* and *Gran Track 10* with at least one of the identified exchange acts: exchange for termination. *Gotcha*, which is also maze-based, features a chase scenario in which a player pursues or is pursued by another player through a shifting landscape. The chase terminates when the pursuer catches the pursued, and the act is then translated into the addition of a recorded point. Simultaneously, a second-by-second record of all cumulative chases is displayed. In this way, the record of linear time brings added context to the point tally, in the sense that it indicates the duration that was required for the total chase tally to accrue. In a game like *Gotcha*, it is possible to see the overarching relevance of temporal order to play, and to see how that order is represented with a pairing of recorded points with an associated chronological record. In one way or another, all the titles identified so far affirm such an order, even though their affirmations may take distinct forms: for example, affirmation through an exchange dynamic or through chronological record keeping, or (as in *Gotcha*) through both.

Individually and collectively, such affirmations designate standards for play in the service of a symbolic order of action and possibility bearing on time. A number of remarkable titles from the 1980s feature interesting experiments with this order—often with exchange opportunities for continuation and termination. In terms of the project at hand, these experiments are particularly exciting when they arrive with aesthetic features that bear on Frye's conception of sentimental romance. With regards to Levine's efforts to identify the so-called building blocks of narrative, the following can be observed: an analysis of such titles and their practices for linking acts of exchange with points can be used to refine conceptions of the fundamental and extraneous dimensions of play. The promise of such work is that it can help determine the significance of individual romantic gestures to specific instances of play. This promise might seem rather irrelevant from a contemporary perspective, as the modern market is awash with videogames that have deep and obvious structural investments in the sentimental romance.[7] However, the marketplace has not always produced titles that have had clear relationships with the sentimental romance (*Pong*, anyone?). Consequently, such analysis stands as an option for digging into the history of the market and specifying subjects and their significance to and for this ancient genre. This work offers nothing less than a revelation of how the genre infiltrated the videogame form. The argument can begin with a consideration of *Pac Man* (1980).

Pac Man's essential scenario—which plays out in a maze—has strong resonances with *Space Race, Gran Trak 10*, and *Gotcha*. However, unlike these titles there is no ticking clock to determine temporal order. However, like *Gotcha*, it does include a running point tally that is based on player action, though this tally is variable and not determined in the sense that it must be correlated with a specific value for play to advance. Rather, it reflects the selective actions of the player as he or she explores the maze to completion. Furthermore, with respect to *Gotcha, Pac Man* iterates on the player's act of play by providing the player with the opportunity to be either the pursued or the pursuer in the context of a single match. For example, at the initiation of play, the player is in the position of the pursued, and the consequence of exchange with a ghost is termination. However, the game also allows for the player to reverse this situation through special cases of exchange associated with select items in the maze. The player can momentarily change his or her position from pursued to pursuer, and in that position complete an act of exchange for continuation with the ghosts. Importantly, these alternative instances of exchange are not equally significant to the player's act of play. For example, while the player's consumption of the ghosts does result in his or her acquisition of points, the act is not technically necessary for the player to complete any given maze. All that is required is that the player avoid exchange for termination. These actions take on special meaning when the title is considered for its associations with Frye's context of romance.

The romantic gesture in *Pac Man* can be initially located in its inclusion of non-representational subjects. These include simply abstract subjects (Pac Man) and subjects with a specific history in the romantic tradition: for example, the ghosts. The ghosts are especially interesting in terms of Frye's commentary on romantic hell as they are quite literally part of the "death-and-rebirth pattern of the underworld."[8] Through their consumption by or termination of Pac Man, the sprites become representatives of the title's illustration of the life and death cycle. Moreover, in both cases they are significant to the concept of "cruelty and horror" as it is played out in this game. These non-representational subjects not only adhere to features associated with romantic hell but also exist in a context that can be associated with romantic hell: the lunatic maze itself. Action unfolds in what is literally an absurd labyrinth, with impossible movement facilitated by the player's traversals beyond the bounds of represented space back into represented space. Moreover, the nature of that action is ritualized and absurd in terms of its evident purpose, which is in the service of repeated maze exploration.

However, it is also true that, just as the sprites, landscape, and action of *Pac Man* associate the game with the romantic night world, they are also evidence that the game is not a literary subject by Frye's standards, as the game plays out entirely within the context of its night world scenario without the interworld experience of ascent or descent. Nevertheless, the title still manages to articulate some very interesting relationships between its romantic figures and spaces, and these relationships can be understood and prioritized in terms of the concepts of exchange for termination and exchange for continuation. The act of play in *Pac Man* includes necessary and optional exchange possibilities, which have distinct meaning for the concept of romance. In terms of play, if Pac Man experiences exchange for termination and is consumed by the ghosts, the death is represented with a special collection of images and sounds, and the player loses one of several possible lives. Alternatively, should Pac Man consume a ghost, there is—significantly—a ritual of added points, and the ghost then "appearing" elsewhere on the map, with animations that do not correlate to the death and resurrection of Pac Man. These outcomes are derived from distinct logical relationships. This difference underscores a context-dependent aesthetics for the death of romantic subjects in *Pac Man*. Notably, under the logic of the game, this aesthetic is either certain or to be avoided for Pac Man during play, but it is essentially optional for the ghosts (though it is very likely to occur in normal play). The motivation for the player to consume the ghosts under optional circumstances can be understood in terms of the act's aesthetic pleasures, which involve the accumulation of additional points.

Here, then, it can be observed that these aspects of the game are essentially interwoven, a notion that is supported under a general consideration of the title. For example, when Pac Man consumes the right power pill and initiates a period where special exchange for continuation is possible, aspects of the game undergo a transformation that brings added context for the aesthetics of ghost death when and if it occurs. The music changes tempo, the color scheme changes, and Pac Man begins to flash wild colors. This distinction creates a meaningful separation between one set of interactions between romantic subjects and another set of interactions between these same subjects. Importantly, these changes are dramatic and superficial to play, and have no actual bearing on the representation of Pac Man's primary goal: the consumption of all the wafers and power pills in the maze. Those wafers and power pills do not change essential point value or purpose when the logic of the title shifts from exchange for termination to exchange for continuation. Moreover, the same can be said of the maze itself, which remains essentially similar except with regards to color. The point here isn't that such changes should be anticipated—rather, the point is that the changes draw a sharp distinction between the features of the game that are significant to the representation of exchange for termination and exchange for continuation, and the latter features are essentially superficial to play. In the logic of the game, the significance of this distinction bears on its implications for points: there are points to be had in *Pac Man* that have no actual bearing on the actions that are required to complete the game.

Subsequent game designers would expand upon the aesthetic and storytelling possibilities of such relations. Arguably, one of the most significant titles in this tradition is *Super Mario Brothers*. Like *Pac Man*, *Super Mario Brothers* has several features that align with Frye's understanding of the "context of romance," but—like *Pac Man*—the game lacks the necessary features to be understood as a proper example of sentimental romance. For example, the title is effectively anti-representational: its associated people, places, and things are fanciful, rather than descriptive of the player's actual world. To the question of whether or not the second significant feature of sentimental romance, the coincidental plot, is relevant to the game, it can be noted that while the actions of the player may adhere to certain logical conditions, the contextualizing scenario that determines his or her interactions with various sprites and challenges is coincidental in the sense that it does not adhere to any evident cause and effect reason at the instance of these interactions: sprites emerge, coins emerge, landscapes emerge, and other features of the game are realized under a rationale that is particular to itself—to be described shortly (and obviously with an eye toward game design).

With regards to the significance of romantic context to the game's potential literary status, it can be noted that Mario appears to move between distinct regions—for example, pastoral landscapes portraying the pragmatic reality of the "Mushroom Kingdom" and underground hellscapes. However, it is also true that the essential challenges and conditions of all these realms are basically the same, and in ways that bind them to the conditions of Frye's night world, a mysterious landscape determined by the absurdity of an essential ritual: Mario's pursuit of the princess through an army of fertility and death spirits. That is, Mario must race through looming Little Goombas, Koopa Troopas, Buzzy Beetles, Cheep-Cheeps, and other monstrous biological forms that threaten death, while seeking out the Magic Mushrooms, Fire Flowers, and Starmans that will strengthen him on his quest. This is his one and only sustained state on his journey to Peach. If, for example, Mario entered a realm of edenic possibility or one that mirrored the world of the player, it would be possible to argue that interworld ascent or descent occurs in the game, but it does not. Consequently, *Super Mario Brothers* is not a literary subject and is not a sentimental romance, but it does present the context of romance, and this context is its definitive condition.

In terms of its evident opportunities for exchange, *Super Mario Brothers* is strikingly similar to *Pac Man*, but with several crucial developments that delimit the boundaries of the game's distinctive "vision of the absurd"—the most significant of which is the inclusion of a time limit for play. Each course must be completed in a certain period, or Mario will expire. However, should the player complete a level in less than the total allowable time, he or she is rewarded with a certain amount of points relative to the amount of time left on the clock. This basic feature of play imbues Mario's presence in the game with special meaning that is not found in *Pac Man*: namely, all actions or non-actions exist in a finite temporal economy, one that has bearing on the player's ultimate score, but which is not necessarily definitive of that score. In *Pac Man*, the significance of wafers and power pills to constructive movement—that is, to movement that brings the player closer to his or her completion of the maze—works to make meaning by endowing select actions with a specific point reward. However, in *Super Mario Brothers* all actions can be associated with a specific point value through an overarching chronological valuation. This essential distinction makes it possible to conclude that the player's presence in the landscape is itself the fundamental determining act for play in *Super Mario Brothers*, and that this presence can be understood as the act of exchange for continuation, wherein time is exchange for two values, one of which is definite but limited—the player's persistence in the world—and the other of which is variable and limited, the total number of points the player can amass by completing a level in a certain amount of time. This scenario presents a firm and specific boundary for gameplay—a constraint, to use Bogost's term—that calls all possible actions into a subordinate relationship with the clock.

Another significant feature of *Super Mario Brothers* that brings special value to the title's experiences of exchange for termination and exchange for continuation is the landscape itself. As is the case in *Pac Man*, *Super Mario Brothers* begins with the player in the vulnerable position of the pursued. Contact with a sprite results in the representation of Mario's death. However, specific conditions, such as the acquisition of a magic mushroom, fire plant, or star, change Mario's basic relationship with the sprites and the outcome of his contact with the sprites in various ways that are bound by the simple fact that contact does not result in Mario's instant death, but in some other outcome. For instance, a "supersized" Mario can run afoul of a sprite and persist in the game space, with the consequence of losing size. A "fiery" Mario can experience the same outcome with the consequence of losing his fire power, and an "invincible" Mario can race along for a certain period and for that period can be impervious to termination if he does not run afoul of the landscape and its limitations (e.g., fall down a hole). Indeed, and significantly, the logic of the landscape always defies the possibility of exchange for continuation and draws one hard limit in the game for the player's possible acts of play: the world cannot be violated without immediate consequence. This is a distinction in kind from the kind of existential horror that is visited on Pac Man, who escapes the maze only to instantly return to it on the other side. The certainty of the landscape in *Super Mario Brothers* is itself a threat to the plumber and his mad dash of fancy. As threat, it exists in lock-step with the clock, which also has the capacity to terminate the player when he or she is in a special condition of exchange for continuation.

Within the confines of this harsh landscape and menacing clock, the player encounters what is tantamount to a game-within-a-game, one which operates under the logic of exchange for continuation, and which engages the very fabric of sentimental romance. Notably, it involves the representation of conspicuous wealth: the game's infamous, enormous "coins." Individually, these coins have value for the player's point score. However, they are also recorded in their own tally, and when the player acquires a specific amount of this form of game capital he or she gains an "extra life." Conceptually, these coins share a great deal in common with the power pills in *Pac Man*—they contribute to a point tally and can provide the player with additional experiential opportunities. However, unlike the power pills in *Pac Man*, they exist in a largely superfluous context, with regards to the necessary actions that advance play. Consequently, their value is closer to that of the ghosts: the player can pursue or not pursue these items, and has finite opportunities to acquire their associated point values in the context of any given level or "maze." This secondary relationship is fascinating for the same reason that ghost consumption was interesting in *Pac Man*: it shows how the game's romantic scenario extends from its fundamental to extraneous features. The essentially optional giant coins share in the same qualities of anti-representation and coincidence that determine the other features of the Mushroom Kingdom, even though their consumption is basically not essential for play. This continuity is important because it speaks to the rigidity of the game's adherence to the context of romance in its major and minor possibilities for play, and thus to the significance of the genre itself to these titles.

However, to speak of *Pac Man* and *Super Mario Brothers* as if these games are internally indicative of their collective romantic features in their entirety would be incorrect, as it would overlook their associated play manuals, or "instruction booklets." For example, the instruction manual for *Pac Man* offers an essential (if absurd) rationale for all the things Pac Man eats: wafers, power pills, ghosts, and vitamins. They are identified as "food" for Pac Man and are to be pursued because they keep him "alive" and "happy."[9] This notion provides a conceptual frame for the game's acts of exchange for termination and continuation—even if that frame is wire-thin. For example, Pac Man's efforts to consume under either set of conditions are in the interests of an apparent biological drive. While this is not a particularly robust explanation for Pac Man's actions, it does bring special meaning to the player's efforts to acquire extra points. Such actions, while they stand beyond what must be completed for the game to advance, link to the larger fantasy of Pac Man's hunger and its satiation. In this way, the acquisition of extra points has value in the game's romantic scenario. This demonstration affirms the identified symbolic order between action and possibility bearing on time to the extent that it is registered in the player's score. Thus, the context of romance endows all capital bearing on the player's score with specific, limited meaning.

Noticeably, a similar determination cannot be made about all forms of capital bearing on the player's score in *Super Mario Brothers*, and the distinction is crucial to understanding the development of the sentimental romance in the videogame form. As was the case with *Pac Man*, the game's instruction booklet provides a brief context for action and possibility bearing on time. However, it reads like a textbook example of Frye's concept of the romance's initiating concern with the descent into poverty.

The description details the Koopa tribe's invasion of the Mushroom people and their kingdom, an act that results in the transformation of the Mushroom people into "stones, bricks, and even field horsehair plants."[10] The player is told that "the only one who can undo the magic spell" is Princess Toadstool who is "presently in the hands of the great Koopa turtle king."[11] Interestingly, the scenario does not account for the giant coins. Are they transformed Mushroom people? Are they simply the wealth of the fallen kingdom that has been distributed helter-skelter across the traumatized world? Is there some other explanation? For example, are they simply features of the Mushroom Kingdom that would have existed prior to the Koopa invasion? Moreover, why is it that they are sitting in the open and waiting for the player to collect them? That is, why are they of no interest to the monstrous biological forms that Mario encounters along his path? The only certain answer is that there is no answer in the text or in the game proper—other than the identification of the coins as "bonus" items—so the coins are and remain literally surreal and mysterious with regards to their origins, though their purpose is definite in the sense that their acquisition has specific implications for the symbolic order of action and possibility bearing on time: that is, in their representation as points, in their representation as part of the coin tally, and in their factoring into Mario's total number of remaining "lives." As such, their significance is—to invoke Bogost's term once again—constrained within the game's second order of gameplay. They generally do not need to be acquired for the player to progress to the end of the game's romantic scenario.

These essential features of the coins—including their lack of context— are like the features of other surreal and mysterious sources of capital in several titles that iterated on *Super Mario Brothers*. Titles like *Sonic the Hedgehog, Donkey Kong Country*, and *Crash Bandicoot* all provide forms of mysterious wealth that escape a rationalizing context other than the context that is provided by the context of romance: these items are essentially anti-representational (either in their depiction or in their world-defying physics) and coincidental to play in their possible valuations and variations. Moreover, like the giant coins, they contribute to the symbolic order of action and possibility bearing on time in their translations into a point tally of one form or another. For example, the rings in *Sonic the Hedgehog* are like the coins in *Super Mario Brothers* to the extent that they are not rationalized within the digital environment in ways that explain their presence. In *Donkey Kong Country*, the bananas scattered across the landscape are rationalized and play a significant part of the instruction booklet narrative. They are the scattered wealth of the land, which Donkey Kong must recover in his efforts to find Diddy Kong. However, in their realization, these bananas, like the coins and rings, are essentially optional for the player to acquire. This notion extends into *Crash Bandicoot*, where the player is promised an economy of mysterious items waiting to be recovered from the game's various crates. Like the coins, rings, and bananas, these items bear on the symbolic order of action and possibility bearing on time in their point translations and other play-determining possibilities, and they are also essentially optional features of play with respect to acts of exchange for continuation or termination.

The persistence of such surreal and mysterious capital across titles suggests Frye's conception of stock images that, he says, make up the metaphorical units of sentimental romance: for example, fertility and death spirits, wild cults chanting it the wilderness, and real or symbolic experiences of ascent or descent, and so on. All of these factor into a larger catalogue of documented images and romantic "metaphors."[12] Considered as such—or as being tangentially relevant to same—these representations of capital can be reconciled with Frye's contention that developmental forms of the sentimental romance will inject seemingly new images—"fabulous" constructions into staid romantic scenarios.[13] However, and importantly, he argues that while such images may seem novel, what they actually represent and address are the deep-seated aspirations and anxieties of their contextualizing cultures. One arrives at this notion only to find Thomas Piketty already there, with his argument that surreal and mysterious conceptions of wealth and the wealthy are to be anticipated broadly within populations during the very years these games were being produced and disseminated to Western audiences.

In this context, it is possible to rationalize such images to other ends. Frye's essential notion that sentimental romance stands on period-specific associations of transhistorical images can be brought to bear on such gameplay to ask whether there is anything about this kind of play in its associations with other subjects that speaks to the unifying concerns of a specific age. For example, just as the program for acquiring extraneous capital in *Super Mario Brothers* is reflected in several subsequent titles, it is also true that these same titles draw from the context of romance in ways that are similar to *Super Mario Brothers*. For example, in terms of Frye's argument, it is interesting to note that *Sonic the Hedgehog, Donkey Kong Country*, and *Crash Bandicoot* play out in a night world scenario: fertility and death spirits bedevil a hero in a landscape of monstrous humanoid forms in ways that project a vision of the absurd. However, and more to the point, in each world, there is one monstrous form (Koopa, Dr. Robotnik, Klump the Kremling, or Dr. Neo Cortex) associated with the beating heart of the game's vision: a nightmare confrontation in the service of exchange for continuation, affirmed for the player in his or her acquisition of a kidnapped individual or individuals. These dramatic scenarios have evident associations with what Frye identifies as the twin concerns of sentimental romance: love and adventure. As such, they collectively represent a stunningly consistent and specific realization of these concerns in the videogame form.

However, such realizations have become less and less significant to videogames since the turn of the millennium, as games of increasing length have become steadily more visible in the market. One interesting feature of this period with respect to the identified acts of exchange and their bearing on capital has been the astounding amount of work that has gone into creating contextualizing rhetoric—or lore—for various forms of capital, often to romanticize the items in ways that underscore their mysterious nature. Before addressing specific examples of this practice, I would like to turn to the concept of lore itself, as it too bears on the sentimental romance and the concept of exchange. For example, if only in a nominal way, the play manuals for *Pac Man* and *Super Mario Brothers* convey something like "lore." That is, they detail the cultural conventions of the fantasy worlds within which the game can be said to occur. Though the descriptions are minimal, they are nevertheless united by an effort to marshal such lore to the point of associating the player with the described environment. This effort affirms Galloway's essential comments on the videogame form as being dependent upon a fundamental effort to reach out in some way to the "social reality of the gamer."[14] In *Pac Man* "you" keep Pac Man happy, and in *Super Mario Brothers* the association is even more explicit: "You are Mario!"[15] This bare-bones context occurs in the service of a larger effort to familiarize the player with the culturally specific knowledge that is required for play: "the rules." Importantly, these rules are rhetorically distinct from the lore, in the sense that they have an inverse function. They relate details that are particular to the world of the player and necessary for the realization of play in their associated digital environment.

The divide between romantic and realist commentary in the play manuals can be bridged with Genettian concepts with special relevance to lore.

In terms of the established argument, it is important to note that lore as such does not present the expansion of exchange—for obvious reasons— but it can nevertheless be recognized as narrative under the following logic. It unfolds in the service of another verb, another action: to quite literally *romance* the reader into the anti-representational and coincidental realities that define the described environment. Select theories from Genette make it possible to assess such romancing on a game-by-game basis, and these assessments can be used to determine the aesthetic concerns of such discourse. With this understanding, it then becomes possible to describe how those concerns bear on actual acts of exchange in the player's act of play.

But to start at the beginning, the use of lore to denote culturally specific knowledge and traditions within videogames narratives can be traced to the Atari instruction manuals, where the romantic elements of play are marshaled as context for play. Similarly, in terms of *Super Mario Brothers, Sonic the Hedgehog, Donkey Kong Country,* and *Crash Bandicoot,* lore is used as such to convey something that might be termed a selective but practical history of the game in question, to the end of involving the player in the romantic world. For example, *Sonic the Hedgehog* establishes the nefarious actions of Dr. Robotnik that have led to Sonic's present journey. In the course of this description, the player and Sonic are transposed through pronoun use: "Help Sonic fight hordes of metal maniacs and do the loop with the Super Sonic Spin attack.... And if you're lucky, you can warp to the secret zone where you spin around in a floating maze!"[16] A similar moment emerges in the description of *Donkey Kong Country* where after a relatively detailed narrative concerning Diddy's kidnapping the player is literally confronted by a cartoon rendering of one of the characters described in the preface matter who says, "You are only reading this because you are bored!"[17] In *Crash Bandicoot,* a slightly different tactic is employed, but it has a similar effect. The player is put in the position of an audience member who is about to hear the story of Crash Bandicoot: "Where were we? Ah, yes —- a hero for our time.... Stick around for the fireworks, the fun is just starting."[18] Here, the first-person plural is used to draw the player into the experience of the game. While the approaches vary, such discourse holds the promise of more than a broadened cultural appreciation for the imagined community under description. It aims to facilitate the player's capacity to imagine him or herself as an actor in a grand—and detailed—narrative that (crucially) always exceeds his or her act of play.

As such, lore establishes an expectation: that all gameplay elements have significance that extends beyond their realization in the immediacy of the player's gaming, and that this significance extends into the historical conditions that undergird play itself. In this context, the player's opportunities to act—his or her various exchanges with contextually significant people, places and things—literally carry the weight of the world and can be conceptualized with various levels of specificity with respect to that world and the contours of the narrative that has been used to romance the reader into that world. To approach this aspect of play, it is necessary to push beyond the special concerns of lore and into the essential content that can be delivered to the player through lore itself.

Genette is useful for such work. Speaking in terms of the role of flashback (or analepsis) in fiction, he considers a range of artistic possibilities for expanding and associating diegetic content—that is, story content. His argument extends from the notion that content is either particular to the established parameters of a given world or contextually distinct with regards to those same parameters. From this position, he speaks of narrative content as being either "homodiegetic" or "heterodiegetic."[19] Homodiegetic content is content that is like or essentially the same as content that has already been established in the narrative, while heterodiegetic content is conceptually distinct from previously established content. For Genette, the essential end of any connection between these categories is to expand upon a represented world. However, such expansions give rise to questions about their contextualizing "voice"—the enunciating entity that draws content into alignment in one fashion or another.[20] Importantly, Genette's chief concern in the consideration of these subjects is their relevance to time: the time of the established content and the time of the added content, and how they are joined through artistic or merely practical methods to facilitate the reader's temporal perspective. With these terms, it is possible to specify the relations between booklet "lore" and the player's act of play. The romancing narrative and the narrative of exchange are homodiegetic, and their contextualizing voice can be identified with the transition out of the romantic narrative and the initiation of the exchange narrative, or vice versa. The temporal concerns of this transition are immediate: the romancing narrative ends with an articulation of the essential conditions that are relevant to the initial act of play in the described environment. Indeed, this time-in-common between the narratives is their shared homodiegetic nexus. In terms of sentimental romance, this temporal value is significant in *Super*

Mario Brothers and similar works for determining crisis—articulating a change that compels the player's initial act of play.

Importantly, this diegetic juncture is entirely superficial to the player's act of play. Beyond the bounds of simple convention and the expectation that the player will want to read the instruction booklet, there is no reason to expect that the player will read lore and come to the game with it in mind, or need it to complete the game. Yet, with respect to these titles and a series of much more developed examples of sentimental romance in the ensuing decade, the larger point is simply the essential gesture: the affirmation of a homodiegetic association that is informative of the player's acts of play in ways that affirm the essential aesthetic conditions of sentimental romance, across narrative structures joined through distinct verbs.

A theory that describes how and why these initially superficial gestures became an increasingly significant aspect of play in the final decade of the twentieth century—and how they became increasingly associated with the representation of capital—can be inferred from additional commentary from Frye and Benedict Anderson. To begin, "lore" in the context of the identified titles demands a homodiegetic perspective: it stands as an elaboration on a definite place, person, or event that the player has or will encounter during normal play (a concept made even more obvious by its association with literal gameplay instructions). By design, then, it anticipates association with gameplay, and as such resonates with Frye's conception of how a narrative universe can emerge from a simple and perhaps isolated fairytale or more developed prose romance. He notes how such works begin in fragmented, transmedia formats and come to "stick together" during normal cultural dissemination.[21] In this way, romantic subjects can establish a potentially massive self-referential system, which would—to use Genette's term—turn on its homodiegetic and heterodiegetic associations and intertextual junctions. The videogame form and its attendant instruction manual stand as an industrial example of this ancient tradition: two discursive forms commenting on the same romantic world, designed to facilitate engagement with a millennia-old process of imaginative world building.

When, as it does for the purposes of this project, that process bears on a cultural anxiety—in this case the estrangement of wealth and the wealthy from everyday life—it is reasonable to ask if there are broader cultural concerns that pre-date the videogame form that may bear on this experience. Benedict Anderson offers a useful theory that can help to guide the investigation of this and similar questions. In *Imagined*

Communities, Anderson considers the chief administrative organs of empire and their physical realization as a sacred space within broad geographies. Drawing from Victor Turner, Anderson notes the significance of a particular act—the act of "journey," between times, statuses, and places as a meaning-creating experience within and between cultures.[22] Under the special conditions of Empire, Anderson attends to the case of "journey as pilgrimage" and makes a key distinction between the significance of a pilgrimage for a pilgrim—in his or her movement to and from a sacred space—and the significance of the pilgrimage to the sacred space itself. Anderson contends that the collective and constant flow of pilgrims moving to such spaces from remote and otherwise unrelated locations works to literally realize the administrative center as a sacred geography, as a conceptual framework for the involved parties.

This conception of empire calls into question the journeys that are illustrated in *Super Mario Brothers, Sonic the Hedgehog, Crash Bandicoot,* and similar titles. Each game presents a pilgrim's literal journey to a seat of administrative power—one that is in a state of despair or one that is in a state of terrifying emergence. As noted, these journeys are essentially romantic in their context. However, with regards to the relevance of that journey to the sacred space itself, new observations can be made. For Anderson, a function of journey for empire is the delineation of the empire's "sacred space," insofar as that space underscores the literal movement to and from such locations. In this context, the boundaries of sacred space would appear when and where the necessity of pilgrim actions undertaken in the service of a goal—the exploration of an administrative center—collide with optional actions, or actions that occur in the service of the pilgrim and not the contextualizing power of empire, necessarily. This is the very space in the identified titles that is occupied by surreal and mysterious representations of wealth, which function in the service of the symbolic order of action and possibility bearing on time, but in ways that affirm the choices of the player over the determined structure of the sacred geography. Interestingly, Frye makes a claim that is like Anderson's when he notes that empires tend to represent themselves in smaller and "smaller units" that stand in reference to —but which lack essential unity with—their empire of origin.[23] He even links engagement with these smaller units and the playful association with same as the necessarily condition for the expression of personal identity in the world (at the expense of empire).

The coins, rings, bananas, and things identified so far play into this larger dynamic, and stand as heralds for what becomes a major concern in gaming at the turn of the millennium: the affirmation of identity in romantic titles through the acquisition of superficial capital. In such titles, the act of exchange is increasingly defined by in-game or real-world purchases, and the player's act of play becomes aligned with notions of class, both in the socioeconomic system determined by the "lore" and by the financial exchanges of the player. Select titles in this tradition are *The Elder Scrolls: Arena* (1994), *Everquest* (1999), and *Diablo* (1996). These titles drive the player towards an "end" as surely as they drive the player to engage with a limited but massive set of opportunities for exchange—to "replay" under the notion that each time the player can choose to make non-essential determinations while visiting again the predictable curves and contours of romance.

Certainly, there were a number of major role playing games for players to choose from before the publication of *The Elder Scrolls: Arena*. However, the game stands as a notable example of the significance of increased choice and its bearing on superficial gameplay to the player's act of play—especially in the form of exchange. First, however, it can be noted that the title shares in the same essential night world concerns that are significant to previous games, starting with *Pac Man*. The subjects are anti-representational and aligned under coincidence. Humanoid forms engage with fertility and death spirits in scenarios bearing on romance and daring-do. However, the game can be distinguished in significant ways from those earlier titles in terms of its relatively extraordinary opportunities for exchange for continuation, the clear majority of which are entirely superficial to play. The significance of such exchange can be noted in the game's character creation opportunities. For example, the game allows the player to select from a range of character classes, each of which comes with determinative features for play. Depending on the selection that is made by the player, he or she will enter the game with certain attributes or possibilities for action that would be denied under other choices. Such actions constitute a form of exchange for continuation. Like the acquisition of points in *Pac Man* or *Super Mario Brothers*, this action has significance for the symbolic order of action and possibility bearing on time. The player's chosen class has temporal implications for what can be done—and how it can be done—in the game. Each class is optional, but all are deterministic to the game—that is, a choice must be made at the expense of other choices.

However, even as the player is making this choice, he or she is confronted with a related but superficial-by-comparison choice: the choice of the character's appearance: that is, "head." The player can select from a small catalogue of "heads" for his or her character and continue with this head into the game. The choice has no bearing on the necessary actions that must be completed for the game to come to its natural conclusion. The distinction between essential and nonessential exchange is significant, as Frye explains that the concept of identity is fundamental to sentimental romance—that is to say, as a definitive concern of romantic narrative, and not merely to the context of romance.[24] Gameplay opportunities like the selection of class and appearance in *The Elder Scrolls: Arena* speak to the emerging significance of curated identity to play (in ways that are distinct from the assertion that the player shares an essential identity with a pre-fabricated character: e.g., "You are Mario!"). With respect to the structure of sentimental romance, this is quite significant, as Frye identifies the hero's confrontation with his or her own identity in the underworld as a key feature of the underworld's vision of the absurd: during his or her experiences in and within the absurd ritual, the hero comes to an ultimate realization of who he or she is.[25]

The essential and inessential identity "customization" dynamic is equally relevant to *Everquest*, which is useful to identify at this juncture because of the ways in which it and *The Elder Scrolls: Arena* share in a general relationship with the representation of capital. Both titles invite the "customized" character to explore the digital environment in the pursuit of larger, directed goals. In his or her wanderings, the player will encounter stashes of represented capital—in the form of various currencies or devices that are required to survive within either game's hostile landscapes. These swords, shields, and other items all bear on the either game's symbolic order of action and possibility bearing on time, to the extent that their acquisition is recorded in the player's "inventory"—a dramatic representation with significance to the concept of the player's score at all points in the game. These items have value in the inventory—even if that value is simply the record of their presence in the inventory. Yet, it is also the case that these values—with respect to the game's definitive features—are extremely limited and are almost always non-essential in any specific combination to play itself.

This observation has relevance for Levine's comments on the roles of "Stars and Passions" in zero-sum games: the possibilities of interacting with a range of personalities in ways that will impact the attitudes of other personalities the player will encounter in the course of play. Under Levine's logic, these interactions would all have value, but the value would not be essential to play, in the sense that any number of interactions and outcomes will lead the player to the conclusion. This understanding of play has evident roots in the inventory systems of games like *The Elder Scrolls: Arena* and *Everquest*, where any number of shields, swords, and magic items might be used to facilitate acts of exchange for continuation or termination in the game world, even though virtually none of the items are, in and of themselves, necessary for the player's act of play.

Diablo is another title that works to underscore the essential insignificance of capital to the player's act of play. It draws from the context of romance, and in that context offers an interesting relationship between currency "coins" and an enormous array of items the player can choose to use (or not use) in many combinations on his or her journey to the high seat of the infernal empire. The items don't invalidate the coin system. Indeed, they are a major part of the coin economy in *Diablo*. However, their randomized placement throughout the world functions as something like a lottery system—a "casino" to use Wark's term—that undermines the general significance of the coin-based economy. Such randomizing occurs in the context of a game where the player can "customize" his or her character in ways that have no actual bearing on the requirements of play: any number of item combinations can lead to the conclusion of the game. However, while the combinations are generally superficial to play, they too contribute to the symbolic order of action and possibility bearing on time through the game's inventory.

The Elder Scrolls: Arena, Everquest, and *Diablo* translate the superficiality of extraneous capital in *Super Mario Brothers* and its many spiritual successors into a much grander superficial inventoried economy, one that speaks to the material excesses of the empires that emerge in each game's night world scenario. These titles speak to the ongoing development of romantic subjects in videogames with acts of exchange for continuation or termination that are superficial to the fundamental components of play but relevant to the definition of the digital environment. In this aesthetic scheme, capital becomes increasingly surreal and mysterious in terms of its practical bearing on the world and absolute values: for example, when a dagger is worth five coins but can also be found in a dead rat and, in any case, is not necessary to play in the first place—then what is its practical value to play?

In terms of these titles, item value has far less to do with the concept of stable capital than it does with the concept of identity. A romantic aesthetic of identity emerges as the player associates his or her "self" with any number of anti-representational gewgaws and other items that emerge from coincidental interactions in the game world. Such identity development is an emerging feature of the symbolic order of action and possibility bearing on time at the end of the twentieth century. While there is no logic to the sentimental romance itself that would determine the development of this aspect of play, Joan Shelley Rubin's theories on American conceptions of gentility and their bearing on popular storytelling structures can be used to explain this phenomenon. As Rubin points out, there is a long-standing assumption in American society that culture and character are intertwined subjects, with the expansion of the former directly benefiting the development of the latter.[26] In these early titles, notions like class arrive with prescriptive implications for the player's act of play within a fantasy culture: they affirm the player's acquisition of items and goods—however meaningless—as efforts undertaken to "develop" a classed entity. Additionally, they facilitate the player's ability to sell goods for in-game currencies, which allows the player to purchase other goods that have essential class implications. Such efforts are productive to the extent that they associate the player with a broader, classed society that stretches beyond the immediate experience of play and into the realm of lore. Here, then, strange and mysterious capital functions in the service of the player's ascension into the higher orders of society in a strange and mysterious world. In this way, videogame exchange fantasies can be identified as cultural expressions with relevance to Thomas Piketty's conceptions of capital and its implications for everyday life at the end of the millennium.

CHAPTER 4

Capital and Class Determinations in Videogames

Abstract Crowley addresses theories of narrative in videogame scholarship. Focusing on observations from Alexander Galloway, Edward Castronova, and David M. Leeson, Crowley attends to scholarly considerations of narrative that fail to define the term. Asserting that Gérard Genette's definition for narrative is essentially compatible with much of what is best in such criticism, Crowley establishes a related argument on the significance of capital and class determinations in videogame narratives from the first decade of the twenty-first century. "Capital and Class Determinations in Videogames" concludes with an assertion that *Halo: Combat Evolved* and *World of Warcraft* illuminate the prime symbolic orders of action and possibility bearing on time that shaped the player's act of play during the millennial period.

Keywords Alexander Galloway · Edward Castronova · David M. Leeson · *Halo: Combat Evolved* · *World of Warcraft* · Class

At the turn of the millennium, several scholars began to address the player's act of play, its conditions, and its broader social implications. Select arguments from within the movement deal with—among other things—the representation of capital in videogames, or with gameplay conditions that have special significance for the concept of capital. Alexander Galloway's "Social Reality and Gaming," Edward Castronova's *Synthetic Worlds: The*

© The Author(s) 2017
A. Crowley, *The Wealth of Virtual Nations*,
DOI 10.1007/978-3-319-53246-2_4

Business and Culture of Online Games, and David M. Leeson's "Northrop Frye and the Story Structure of the Single-Player Shooter" are indicative of the major commentaries from the period that have special relevance to the project at hand. In its own way, each argument brings added context to the concept of a symbolic order of action and possibility bearing on time. However, it is also true that these works share in the challenging conceptualization of "narrative" that troubles many commentaries from the period: that is, a conceptualization that does not stand on an actual definition for the term. Consequently, the authors' capacities to comment on related literary subjects, such as symbols, are quite limited. Nevertheless, it can be said with some certainty that select arguments in these and related texts rise above (or at least manage) this central limitation in the service of a significant, general claim.

Galloway's "Social Realism in Gaming" is particularly impressive in this regard. The argument makes heavy use of the term "narrative," even though the term is never defined. For Galloway, "narrative" appears to have no special meaning, though the term is frequently associated with other, more definite concepts: for example, "fictional narrative," "realistic narrative," "narrative of normal life," "protorealist anxiety narrative," "a certain type of narrative," "militaristic narrative," and so on.[1] In such combinations, "narrative" seems to designate a category of something—some variable, which is shaded in mysterious ways by an attendant quality, theme, or concern. However, there is at least one moment in the argument when Galloway strikes upon a vision of narrative with some substance. When writing about *State of Emergency*, he describes the "narrative itself" as "a fantasy of unbridled, orgiastic anti-corporate rebellion."[2] If that phrase is boiled down to its operative verb, "rebellion," something like a potential exploration of the game as an expansion into a larger "fantasy" can be anticipated, and even hypothetically pursued under the question of how the exchange possibilities identified so far might contribute to this fantasy, to say nothing of the potential contributions to (or refutations of) the sentimental romance that may emerge during the player's act of play.

However, to the more pressing question of how Galloway's larger argument might be associated with the project at hand, it is useful to begin with an obvious limit to the author's analytical scheme. He identifies *State of Emergency* as an example of "social realism" in gaming, and defines the concept in broad terms: "To find social realism in gaming one must follow the tell-tale traits of social critique and through them uncover the beginnings of a realist gaming aesthetic."[3] With regards to the anticipated "realist gaming aesthetic," Galloway simply does not have a vocabulary on-hand to discuss this aesthetic—or any aesthetic—in detail, but he does hypothesize its existence and does provide an excellent example of what this aesthetic might look like in the wild. For example, in *State of Emergency* the game instructs "players to 'smash the corporation' and then gives them the means to do so.'" In this way, he contends, the game generates a social critique on corporate structures that exist beyond the player's act of play. In addition—and more usefully—he considers circumstances surrounding an earlier title, *Toywar*. The goal of the game is to "fight against the [real-world] dot-com toy retailer http://eToys.com by negatively effecting their stock price on the NASDAQ." In their early game playing, he contends, gamers brought attention to the actual corporation that is represented in the title and were instrumental in its actual real-world downfall. Whether this essentially unsubstantiated claim is true, the notion that the game anticipates a collapse that came to pass in the actual market is interesting. Indeed, I see no real need for the game to have been an actual part of the corporation's dissolution for the larger point to remain sound: *Toywar* is an anecdotal example of social commentary with real-world associations for the player in his or her act of play.

Interestingly—with regards to the specific temporal conditions that assumedly made *Toywar*'s message relevant to http://eToys.com, Galloway argues that social realism in gaming requires that the game and the player share a political congruence with regards to the title's "realism" before the experience of social realism will be realized in the player's act of play.[4] He defends this point with a laundry list of militaristic shooters from the period—*America's Army, Special Forces, Under Ash*, and *SOCOM*—and argues that each title's latent social realism is dependent upon a political situation that is assumedly shared by the player. It is an interesting argument to the extent that it suggests a potential (and potentially widespread) purpose for gaming that is contextually bound by the personal politics of the player. As such, it anticipates a consideration of games and gaming that is far more granular than the project at hand, which has taken the wide, stable shadow of sentimental romance itself—a subject that stands apart from the contingent politics of the moment and, rather, lords over the horizon of human history. This is precisely why Galloway's argument is so useful—it reminds one of the contingent nature of the player him or herself, and of his or her ability to value the act of play with regards to his or her own life. In terms of Frye, the notion has special relevance to the construction of "fabulous" sentimental romance, works that call the seemingly unique cultural aspirations and anxieties of the moment into the service of a narrative of love or adventure, or both.[5]

However, it is also true that Galloway's claim of political congruence leads him to what is from the perspective of this project a conceptual dead end. Too enthusiastically, he argues that social realism in gaming is a very new development. He writes, "Forty years of electronic games have come and gone and only now does one see the emergence of social realism."[6] The claim is certainly debatable, particularly when all of the identified titles are considered for their exchange opportunities—their very language for communicating with the player—which extend backward into the video-game form's romantic past. Yet, regardless of whether one agrees with Galloway's view of the historical significance of social realism or not, his argument is interesting in that it suggests the conditions of the day may bear on the title and its constituent features to the end of creating cultural frisson—either conceptually or through the instigation of action in the larger world.

In terms of the argument at hand, this position can lead to the question of whether a congruence of political concerns bearing on social realism can extend to the manifestation of capital within games, as well as other subjects. Edward Castronova supports this notion and details how it might actually come to pass. In *Synthetic Worlds: The Business and Culture of Online Games, Exodus to the Virtual World*, and *Wildcat Currency*, he explores the ways in which early twenty-first-century considerations of wealth have left their indelible stamp on the player's experience of play. However, like Galloway, Castronova tends to talk about narrative without using an actual definition for the term, and this is important to the extent that one must be provided before it is possible to comment on how his claims bear on my proposed scheme. Fortunately, it is also true that he uses the term with a consistency that is indicative of at least a general meaning for the concept. In *Synthetic Worlds*, he uses the term sparingly: for example, "interesting and enjoyable narrative," "little narratives," "rags-to-riches narratives," and "narrative realism."[7] As was the case with Galloway, in each instance "narrative" has a function not all that dissimilar to tofu: it provides bland texture for an associated concept. Importantly with regards to Frye and Genette, virtually all of these examples emerge in the context of Castronova's reflection on action: that is, gamers "drive" an "interesting and enjoyable narrative," rags-to-riches narratives are valued for the opportunities they provide for the player to "do" something, and "narrative realism" is determined by "interesting and extraordinary numerous quests."[8]

While Galloway and Castronova present conceptions of narrative that at least lean in the direction of verbal development, it is also apparent that the two have distinct conceptions of the significance of the player's political situation with regards to his or her experience of "narrative realism"—social or otherwise. Galloway's comments on the variables that underlie "congruence" are not all that significant to Castronova. For example, rather than view the experience of play as a potential alignment of player politics with the political position of a game, Castronova views such as an extension and affirmation of a global economic reality: capitalism itself. Certainly, there is room within the argument for various commentaries on capitalism, but Castronova does not make such commentaries a subject of his work. Rather, he speaks of what he regards as the essential conditions of play in synthetic worlds. He writes, "The avatar's stock of experience points, skills, and possessions is a capital stock, just like capital stocks on Earth. Possessions are like physical capital, and avatar skills and experience levels are like human capital. There, as here, investments in capital stock increase the power."[9] You can literally "buy avatar capital, for real money."[10]

With regards to *Super Mario Brothers* and other titles that pre-dated the rise of the kinds of massive online games discussed in *Synthetic Worlds*, it is interesting to note that Castronova links acquisition to the experience of action variables. He writes of "advancement systems" that "involve the enhancement of the avatar's physical or nonphysical capital as a consequence of specific actions."[11] He goes on to explain that such actions lead to "physical capital" such as "money and armor" and "[n]on Physical capital" like "experience points and skill ratings and attribute enhancements."[12] Tellingly, he links the action possibilities of advancement systems with an essential assumption about the significance of capitalism to the player's act of play and writes that "capitalism loves to explore."[13] The claim is noteworthy in that it associates the economic system with a basic verb: explore (and also love, no less). As noted, the sentimental romance provides a ready landscape for explorations that occur in the service of its thematic investments in love and adventure. The notion that modern games marshal capitalistic tendencies into romantic spaces is noteworthy.

This point also speaks to the horizon of Castronova's argument: that is, "advancement systems" and "avatar capital" are discussed essentially in the context of massive online games. While Castronova never implies these concerns are not relevant in earlier offline titles, his argument works to present these conditions as a special circumstance of the games he considers. One feature of his argument, then, is the implication that these concepts are very new to games, just as Galloway sees social realism as being essentially particular to the turn of the millennium. A review of the sentimental romance as it manifests in games from the 1970s, 1980s, and 1990s belies these notions, insofar as the various point systems can be read as avatar capital with relevance to symbolic orders of action and possibility bearing on time. However, it is the case that Castronova's useful conceptions of "advancement systems" and "avatar capital" are welcome terms that help to specify my own argument.

A related, noteworthy effort to bring Frye into the context of such conversations is launched by David M. Leeson. Like Galloway and Castronova, Leeson suffers from an underdeveloped conception of narrative—which is tragic, given his investment in Frye. The author writes of "different narrative modes," a "master narrative . . . of regeneration through violence," of a "kind of narrative," or "romantic narrative," "game narratives," and "metanarratives."[14] As was the case with Castronova, the notion of "conceptual tofu" once again comes to mind: the term seems to be essentially featureless, and takes on definition in relation to some other concept. However, unlike Castronova or Galloway, there is no single use of the term in the document that would allow the reader to rationalize its association with Frye—other, of course, than the simple assertion on Leeson's part that the concept simply carries across the media that are included in his argument, including videogames. This is meaningful because Frye himself does not provide a rationale for considering the sentimental romance beyond the horizon of prose narrative, generally. Consequently, a coupling rationale is required to move Frye's theories beyond the limits of Frye's own light.

However, while Leeson struggles to contextualize his argument, it is the case that his claims are often noteworthy of review and prime for development in the present period. He makes the appreciable observation that many "first-person shooter" titles dramatize what Frye identifies as basic features of the sentimental romance. Leeson notes the relevance of this genre to titles as divergent as *Halo: Combat Evolved, Max Payne, Half-Life 2, Killzone, F.E.A.R., Painkiller, DarkWatch, Halo 2, Max Payne 2, The Suffering, Doom 3*, and *Quake 4*. Throughout, his relationship with Frye is highly selective, associative, and assumptive. Leeson selects key concepts from Frye's grand theories of romance—such as the famous commentary on the eternal feminine, mode and mythos, violence and cunning, and then associates them when and where it is plausible to do so in his consideration of each title, without apparent context, and without engaging Frye's theories about why it is that the sentimental romance spreads from culture to culture in the first place.

With respect to Galloway, the argument and its fallacies bring special attention to the first-person shooter, and in particular to the fantasy first-person shooter. For example, do—or can—*Halo: Combat Evolved* and the other titles that do not share in a real-world military scenario contribute to "social realism"? Under Galloway's assessment, they would not, as their political position is essentially fanciful. However, under Leeson's argument, they would, to the extent that they take on the storytelling values of the sentimental romance, which are surely part and parcel of the gamer's social situation, and translate them into the experience of play. It is the special contention of this project that an excellent conceptual link for yoking works of supposed social realism with works with significance to the sentimental romance is the symbolic order of action and possibility bearing on time—which can be associated with Castronova's concept of avatar capital, the symbolic record that constitutes what Levine elsewhere describes as the "smallest units of narrative" in the videogame form.

A bounded horizon for such inquiry would be the context of romance and/or the development of same into appreciably more refined examples of sentimental romance. The point would be to attend to the various aesthetic schemes that have been used to realize these narrative concerns across time. For the purposes of this project, those schemes are realized in acts of exchange: for termination, for continuation, and for stasis. With regards to the new millennium and the years in advance of the Global Great Recession, it is hard to imagine a more appropriate title for such inquiry than *Halo: Combat Evolved*. As a shooter, it offers ready association with Galloway's comments on the significance of a definite social position with regards to social realism. In the context of that argument, the title would appear to not be an example of social realism, as it could not be aligned with the experiential realities of the player beyond the game itself. With respect to Castronova, the game's advancement systems speak to the fluid, variable, and limiting values of avatar capital, and to the essential conditions of such advancement as they existed prior to the mainstream emergence of what Castronova dubs synthetic worlds. This notion, in the context of Galloway, can lead to the observation that—regardless of the title's investment in real-world social situations, it advances a notion of capital that is significant to the experience of the game. With regards to Leeson, it is reasonable to ask how this presentation of capital plays into the title's larger investment in sentimental romance—and an extended night world scenario wherein Master Chief races through mazes and battles with absurd humanoid forms that determine the game's experience of fertility (health) and death. Moreover, and with regards to the project at hand, all of this can then be situated against the question of how these concerns find their expression in acts of exchange realized in the title's symbolic order of action and possibility bearing on time.

From this, it is possible to identify a dimension to avatar capital that is distinct from the representations of avatar capital in previously considered titles. In *Halo: Combat Evolved,* the player's interactions with capital are a much more significant aspect of his or her act of play than they are in *Super Mario Brothers* and *Sonic the Hedgehog.* Various weapons, ammunitions, and health packs work to define Master Chief's inventory in ways that bear directly on the experience of play moment by moment, and in ways that determine immediate possibilities for action. Consequently, the inventory—and by extension the assumed identity of Master Chief—is a subject of constant concern for the player, who must acquire and organize avatar capital to meet the needs of the present and the anticipated needs of the future. In this hyper-determined atmosphere, exchange for continuation with avatar capital takes on the features of exchange for stasis: that is, there is a certain amount of inventory that must be retained for the player to simply persist in his or her journey through the game. That amount is variable and context dependent, but it is necessarily a meaningful part of play—just as the introduction of the clock to *Super Mario Brothers* brought added context to the symbolic order of action and possibility bearing on time. In *Halo: Combat Evolved,* the player "must have" capital to not only continue, but simply to remain an active agent within the world. Surely, the player can exist in the world without the required means to advance, but advancement always requires the acquisition and expenditure of new avatar capital.

This is not a traditional feature of the sentimental romance. Capital, as such, surely is, to the extent that interworld ascent or descent is dependent upon the action of the hero as he or she encounters the people and items that facilitate his or her journey. But the notion that the act of acquiring itself is an existential condition of the romantic scenario stands apart from the traditional genre—and so, in terms of Frye's argument, it can be identified as a "fabulous" construction relevant to the videogame form in such works. Importantly, with regards to Piketty, the need to acquire avatar capital is not optional in *Halo: Combat Evolved*. The player must do so to persist, and in this way can be identified as being in a constant state of debt with regards to his or her inventory and the experiential opportunities that this inventory will afford him or her during play.

Indeed, this relationship is symbolic of the experience of debt in a way that is significant to the sentimental romance: that is, it bears on identity. How Master Chief is comported to persist at all given moments is a prime concern in play. One of the more interesting aspects of this play is its larger significance for notions of family. Master Chief is in a constant scramble to save his "fellow soldiers," who contribute to the game's advancement system to the extent that they provide both added firepower and—interestingly—constant compliments that affirm the identity of Master Chief. This basic relationship can be found in all the military titles that Galloway identifies, both in the works of supposed social realism and the works of fanciful play. This basic set of circumstances, a hero in a debt relationship with the experiential opportunities of narrative, as recorded and determined by avatar capital in an advancement system, has an important role in the pre-Recession "synthetic worlds" that are so central to Castronova's arguments, and to arguments he would go on to make in later, equally notable works.

With widening eyes, one might note that these conditions emerge in the context of a first-person shooter with militaristic overtones. With regards to avatar capital, this is significant to the extent that all capital that flows through the game bears on either the human or alien militaries, within which there are clear rank divisions baked into the relevant social hierarchies (the head of the Covenant is literally called "the Hierarch"). However, these divisions have little to no significance for when, where, and who might have access to different forms of avatar capital, other than the sharp distinction that divides human use of alien technology in all cases except for the special case of Master Chief. As such, Master Chief stands as a unique vector through which all the riches of this weird little drama can flow. It is a distinguishing characteristic that speaks to his (literally) larger identity within the military organization.

From this, it is interesting to note that subsequent titles that would iterate on such exchange would go on to generate worlds with very specific rules and conditions bearing on advancement systems. This work appears in the interests of establishing class boundaries in game worlds. Certainly, such designations existed prior to this period, as is evidenced, for example, by *The Elder Scrolls: Arena*. However, in a game like *World of Warcraft* the initial context of play is not the traditional romantic concern with ascent or descent, but rather the fabulous addition of the identity question, with all of its attendant implications for exchange for continuation and the reality of gameplay debt as recorded in the advancement system's symbolic expression in the player's' inventory of avatar capital. Unlike Master Chief, the played character in *World of Warcraft* represents one market experience that is distinguished from a finite set of other experiences by "class restrictions": certain items cannot flow into and out of certain players.

While all possible avatar capital contributes to exchange for continuation in a game like *World of Warcraft*, it also contributes to the experience of capital as surreal and mysterious to the extent that the game lacks non-class-based explanations for why so much capital in the game is "out of bounds." The notion that one character does not have a certain kind of capital because it is not his or hers to have exists in a near-perfect overlay with the modern notion that wealth is not to be acquired by the average individual because it is not his or hers to have—because it is reserved for others by the system itself. Importantly, the inventory logic in a game like *World of Warcraft* is essentially defined by this central assertion. Interestingly, the logic makes no determinations based on the relative value of the involved items within the game world: a two-copper coin item or a ten-gold coin item can be equally beyond the player's reach, simply because of the game's classed logic for wealth. In this way, an important connection can be made with Piketty's argument, as it assumes that the exchange value of wealth is what places it beyond the ken of so many contemporary people. With regards to *World of Warcraft*, the value-blind class system is extremely effective in affirming the notion that the experience of surreal and mysterious wealth cuts across all people, places, and things: it is the very foundation of the game's classed perspective. It confronts capitalistic notions of acquisition and expenditure with what amounts to the absurd ritual of class affirmation, performed in the service of the game's conceptual and experiential boundaries.

The rise of such play—with its attendant notions of debt and identity—establishes novel ground for the videogame form to engage the context of romance. It also provides insight into what appears to be a major trope in videogames for delineating the experience of ascent or descent. For example, *Halo: Combat Evolved* can be said to draw from the context of romance, but to not be an actual example of such romance as it does not detail any actual interworld ascent or descent (it includes such actions superficially in its opening and closing segments), and by Frye's determination is more closely aligned with the concept of the Fairy Tale.[15] However, and as was the case in *The Oregon Trail*, *World of Warcraft* creates various gameplay experiences, where the conditions of play are appreciably distinct from one another: for example, with various settlements and their attendant shopping experiences. The relevance of such experiences stretches all the way back to *The Legend of Zelda* and beyond, to be sure, to *The Oregon Trail*. This pattern provides structure to the sentimental romance as it emerges in the videogame form. However, as the period of the Global Great Recession approaches this pattern begins to undergo notable changes that themselves have special bearing on the rise of surreal and mysterious wealth in everyday life. These changes are new evidence of the videogame form's developing—and now longstanding—commentary on class boundaries.

CHAPTER 5

Night World Identity Affirmations

Abstract Crowley considers gamer identity and its relationship to representations of wealth in videogames. Drawing from McKenzie Wark, Ian Bogost, and Nick Dyer-Witheford and Grieg de Peuter, Crowley posits that Frye's conception of the hero in the underworld has special bearing on the player's act of play in titles from the period of the Global Great Recession. Highlighting the significance of surreal and mysterious wealth in such tales to the final affirmation of the hero's identity, Crowley examines the relevance of player inventory systems to the concluding moments of *BioShock* and *Mass Effect*—both of which underscore the illusion of player choice at the same moment they affirm the hero's identity.

Keywords McKenzie Wark · Ian Bogost · Nick Dyer-Witheford · Grieg de Peuter · *BioShock* · *Mass Effect*

Galloway, Castronova, and Leeson offer broad perspectives on games and gamers that intersect over general notions of ideological continuity: for example, a continuity between the player's socioeconomic conditions and the social commentary of a game (Galloway), a continuity between broad capitalist perspectives stemming from the player and the developer (Castronova), and a continuity between the ancient literary genre of sentimental romance and the genre of the first-person shooter (Leeson).

© The Author(s) 2017
A. Crowley, *The Wealth of Virtual Nations*,
DOI 10.1007/978-3-319-53246-2_5

These assumptions facilitate analytical programs with various levels of specificity: that is, Galloway takes the abstract possibilities of player and game "congruence" as his prime subject of consideration, while Castronova takes capitalism itself as the operative field for the player's act of play—and Leeson surveys a short list of de-contextualized structural components and uses them as the boundary points for his argument. The individual arguments are exciting, and their intersecting concerns are even more so, insofar as they rest on questions about the essential relationship between the player and the game, and the extent to which that relationship is itself a delimiting feature of the act of play. Therefore, each theory leads to questions about what a gamer is and how the act of play can impact gamer identity. At the same time, none of these theories land on a specific conception of these subjects, other than the conceptions that are particular to their analytical programs. This is not a shortcoming for any of the individual authors, but it does pose a challenge for any program seeking to align such observations over a stable conception of either games or the gamer's act of play.

Fortunately, there are theories from the same period that define these concepts and which are also compatible with many of the productive observations in Galloway, Castronova, and Leeson. For example, McKenzie Wark and Ian Bogost establish essential conceptions of these subjects. For his part, Wark provides a specific conception of the early twenty-first-century gamer, one that has significance to Piketty's notion of economically degraded populations. Bogost provides an equally useful consideration of the gamer's act of play and works to establish a conceptual frame for addressing how it is that games communicate with players, and players with games. His work too has special significance for Pikettian concepts in the context of actual gameplay scenarios.

Yet, while Wark and Bogost bring added context to the argument at hand, it is also the case that they too struggle with the concept of narrative in ways that must be addressed before their theories will be significant to the symbolic order of action and possibility bearing on time. Fortunately, it is quite possible to resolve these issues with Genette's conception of narrative. For example, in *Gamer Theory*, Wark presents a very challenging understanding of "narrative." At certain points, he writes as if he has a conception of "narrative" in mind: for example, "Narrative is just another kind of interface."[1] Unfortunately, what that means, exactly, is never discussed. At other points, the curious notion that "narrative structure" is a concept with specific currency that somehow unites varied and famously complicated critical perspectives—for example, the perspectives of Adorno, Debord, Baudrillard, and even Plato—is simply presented as a given.[2] Elsewhere, other instances of the term emerge that lead to significant questions about connotation and denotation. For example, the reader is directed to see the work of J.C. Herz "for a narrative account of the intertwining of military and entertainment industries."[3] What, one wonders, is a narrative account? By Wark's own reasoning is it an "interface account?" Would Adorno agree with that? Would Baudrillard? Later, Wark makes a similarly vague reference to a "transhistorical narrative form," and one can only imagine Plato shaking his famously ugly head in confusion.[4] From all of this, it can be concluded that the term has basically no specific value in the argument, other than to indicate the author's self-assurance that he is using the term to some effect. It is as if he is speaking a mysterious twin language without the benefit of a twin. Perhaps the best evidence that the term has no real meaning in the argument comes when the author draws uncritically from the work of Patrick Dugan, who writes, "A story in a game is an embedded narrative that is always parallel to agency."[5] This is a distinction without a difference, insofar as neither story nor narrative means anything particular in the claim, or in the context for the claim.

However, while the term itself comes to no useful use in the argument, it is also true that the way in which it is used is very telling, and speaks to what is most interesting in *Gamer Theory*: for example, the totally desperate position of the game theorist. Wark is attentive to and critical of what he identifies as the absolutely blind certainty of the modern gamer with respect to the supposed form and functions of games, a relationship he illustrates with an interesting (if somewhat problematic) partial appropriation of Plato's famous "Allegory of the Cave," which leads to the notion that the gamer imagines him or herself in a world that is entirely defined by game logic.[6] Wark uses the allegory to define the ontological position of a hypothetical game theorist as he or she begins to press past game logic and into broader possible experiences that will bring added context to such logic. In the context of desperate theorists grasping in the dark, the curious use of "narrative" in *Gamer Theory* speaks to the assumedly isolated and uninformed position of the mole-eyed game theorist as he or she struggles to articulate a broader understanding of the world of games in the context of the world itself. In this sense, the usage should not be criticized so much as it should be rescued as quickly as possible—or at least aligned with a sound definition from the broader world the game theorist is eager to join, and where he or she is now most welcome.

However—and regardless of whether one takes Wark's hyperbolic commentary on the blind certainty of the gamer seriously (and there is good reason not to, as it effectively presents the gamer as a creature out of time and space)—the more important and larger point from this work is that the gamer has become effectively dissociated from his or her surety of "the real" in the modern period by the algorithms of game logic itself— whatever that phrase might entail. This broad theory and essential situation establishes a general opportunity to consider how gamers and game theorists might conceive of wealth and the wealthy if their conceptions of these subjects were truly bound to videogame gameplay experiences. Under Wark's reasoning, the symbolic order of action and possibility bearing on time takes on special relevance, as its exchange logic—for example, for termination, continuation, or stasis—presents limited, boundary concepts for specifying game logic within and between titles, to the end of shaping the gamer's perspective. Insofar as such logic has an appreciable investment in the context of romance and an appreciable role in the history of the videogame form, a consideration of it as an extension of the romantic genre provides one path (of presumably many potential paths) away from Wark's zit-warming gaming monitor and toward potential full-face illumination—with branching paths leading to and through Galloway, Castronova, and Leeson.

However, it is also true that such a journey requires a conceptual leap— from the abstract state of the gamer to the concerns of the identified theorists and critics. Fortunately, it is possible to construct a bridge to these logical concerns with arguments drawn from Ian Bogost's *Persuasive Games: The Expressive Power of Videogames*. While Wark makes the ontological conditions of the gamer his prime concern, Bogost makes the discursive features of the game and gamer relationship itself his subject of inquiry. It is a useful effort for several reasons, one of which is that it challenges the notion that the gamer is somehow an entity out of time and space—a weirdo floating in the void—and is instead a subject that can be accounted for under the broad and ancient subject of rhetoric. Bogost describes his work as an "analysis of the way videogames mount arguments and influence players" and explains that it extends from a central contention that there is a distinction with a difference between rhetoric understood as oratory and "a new domain for persuasion [in videogames], thanks to their core representational mode, procedurality."[7]

Unlike other critics who have been considered so far, Bogost gestures toward a definition for "narrative," though the gesture is of limited value to Bogost's actual argument, and does more harm than good. For example, the only indication of a definition for "narrative" emerges in an excerpt the author provides from Plato's *Phaedrus*. In that excerpt, Bogost indicates that Socrates uses the term "diegesis" for "narrative." In his elucidation of this passage, Bogost indicates that diegesis can be understood as "a description or narration of events."[8] Instantly, the question of how one squares "a description or narration of events" with "narrative" emerges: for example, are "description" and "narration" synonymous, and—perhaps more pressingly—what does it mean for either term to have an existence beyond the subject—that is, the "events"—they recount?

Before moving on, it is worth noting that Plato provides a much more refined—and limited—concept of diegesis in *The Republic*, where it is paired with the concept of mimesis. There, the term indicates the telling of a tale by a narrator, while *mimesis* is an imitative act that shows rather than tells.[9] When Bogost uses the term "diegesis" to indicate "a description or narration of events," he is using the term in ways that are indeed consistent with Socrates—but—importantly—only in the sense that Socrates is referencing the act of a narrator telling a tale, which is not the same as the tale considered as its own subject of inquiry, one that contains the telling of the tale but which is also subject to the rhetorical conventions of the telling and the medium through which the tale is delivered. Or, to simply use Genette's observation, the narrative is the text itself and should be recognized as such to avoid terminological confusion.

Bogost's confusion of "narration" with "narrative" ripples throughout the text. He speaks of "narrative fragments," literally speaks of narrative as a general "descriptive account," identifies a mysterious "very particular linear narrative of tragic drama," indicates "narrative gestures," and attempts to distinguish videogames from "narrative media." At one point, he claims that a "narrative plays with moral ambiguity," and late in the text identifies a "narrative summary."[10] In each instance, the term bears on the notion that a communication is taking place, but that communication has no actual edges or definite features, and this is because this use of narrative as such has no fundamental grounding in a contextualizing concept. This problem vanishes if the term "narration" is substituted in each instance, as the term indicates that the concept emerges from a narrative, which then awaits definition (though it never arrives). However, Bogost uses the word "narrative"—not narration—and, thus, questions about the actual source and its conceptual boundaries are forever challenging his statements. With regards to the challenges of the so-called ludology/narratology debates that defined the era during which *Persuasive Games* was published, it is important to note that the exact problem that challenges Bogost's argument was identified nearly forty years before by Genette, who noted not only widespread confusion within narratology in the 1970s between narrative, narration, and narrator, but also—with respect to Bogost—within the Platonic dialogues as well.[11]

Yet, while there are some significant challenges for the concept of narrative in *Persuasive Games*, it is also the case that Bogost makes some very interesting comments on the personal politics of players and capital that can be used to link Wark's scrambling game theorist with the work of Alexander Galloway and Edward Castronova. Moreover, his comments have special relevance to several significant questions that arise in the work of David M. Leeson. With regards to Galloway, Bogost indicates that any perceived "congruence" between the gamer and game's evident political situation must be tempered by the fact that procedural representations "often do not allow the user to mount objections through configurations of the system itself."[12] The point is useful, and should remind the player that while a game may appear to argue for a certain form of social critique or action, the rules of play limit how such action can be imagined or performed within the game. Or, to put it another way, the game can speak to the gamer, but the gamer cannot speak to the game—or at least not in ways that exceed the procedural logic of the game.

It is a useful concept to the extent that it transforms the gamer, game, and the binding social situation loop that is relevant to Galloway's understanding of the videogame form into a hierarchy with regards to a game's efforts to transmit a political perspective. The point here is not that such a hierarchy would invalidate Galloway's central claims. Rather, the point is that Bogost provides a context for discussing scenarios where the perspective of the game and perspective of the gamer fail to achieve frisson: the operative boundary concept is the game's procedural logic, not its immediate and obvious political concerns, which might be relevant to any player—conceivably—insofar as the game provides a means for the player to communicate a response to those concerns that is significant to the player and his or her social position. As Wark's hypothetical gamer lacks any perspective other than the transmitted perspective of game logic, he or she can be established at the bottom of this hierarchy as a perfect receptacle for the game's options for political discourse. Such an entity is—of course—absurd, but it does establish an essential condition for Wark's gamer: he or she is receptive to game logic, and that receptivity is dependent upon his or her ability to affirm it in the act of play.

This notion can draw attention to the symbolic order of action and possibility bearing on time, and lead to questions about how it is that the player goes about constructing a record of play through something like an inventory. And it is at this moment that the concept of procedural rhetoric moves beyond the limits of political possibility and into the less-determined realm of aesthetics: for example, how do patterns of exchange for continuation, termination, or stasis individually and collectively bear on the symbolic order and the player's relationship with that order? Bogost edges toward this question in his comments on the similarities between *America's Army* and *A Force More Powerful*. Unlike Galloway, he does not view a game like *America's Army* as expressing a definite political situation waiting to be paired with a bright-eyed American youth. Rather, Bogost notes that both it and *A Force More Powerful* "accentuate the incompleteness and complexity of political situations." He continues, "While these games offer holistic models that attempt to explain intricate political situations through a single logic, other procedural arguments attempt to highlight the causal or associative connections between see-mingly atomic issues."[13] The notion of multiple logics at work within a single game is useful to the extent that it raises questions about the interpretive possibilities of game logic, and whether or not it should ever be assumed that the procedural arguments in a given title all work in the service of a master thesis. This has significance to the arguments of Wark, Castronova, and Leeson, insofar as it calls their readings in the service of ideologically pure subjects—the imaginary gamer, a totalizing capitalist enterprise, or the looming sentimental romance—into question: for example, are there aspects of the player's act of play that might either challenge, avoid, or simply compromise the player's ability to recognize these assumedly determinative subjects?

To this point, Bogost makes a number of interesting comments about the significance of procedural rhetoric to capital in one of the last major pre-Recession titles: *The Sims* (2000), which is a subject of special interest for both Wark and Castronova. For his part, Wark notes that "Games redeem gamespace by offering a perfect unfreedom, a consistent set of constraints."[14] In a game like *The Sims*, these constraints are envisioned as a "meter," one that demands that the player take part in interwoven life and commerce cycles. Wark notes, "[T]he meter is always running. It is integral to gamespace, if not necessarily to what makes gamespace possible."[15] Here, the notion of "perfect unfreedom" is of special value to the hypothetical cipher-gamer, as it presents him or her with an assumedly ideal system of meaning. Whether or not this assumption has any relevance to an actual person with more complicated notions of freedom is for the moment not that important. Rather, the central logic of Wark's claim is what is significant—the notion that the gamer seeks out a totalizing system and, thus, willingly places him or herself at the bottom of a hierarchical relationship with the game logic of *The Sims*. Usefully, Castronova points out that one evident outcome of player's playing *The Sims*—in this instance *The Sims Online* (2002)—is that the act of play provides an opportunity for many players to live out repressed sexual fantasies. He writes, "*The Sims Online* suggests that when users have complete freedom to build their avatars and their homes, they often build erotic playgrounds and girls and embed them in fetish playgrounds. Literally."[16] Unfreedom for Wark's gamer is freedom for Castronova's, and Bogost's logic makes it possible to talk about how the outcomes of either experience are the same. Rather than conclude that sexual fantasies—or any fantasies—that arise from the player's act of play are indicative of the player's mind and desires, Bogost's logic would indicate that these outcomes are first and foremost dependent upon the finite, bounded opportunities that are provided to the player by the game. Thus, any perceived desires from the subconscious are only realized because they are allowed under the game's procedural logic.

The rise of *The Sims* and *The Sims Online* at the same time as *World of Warcraft* in the popular imagination speaks to the significance of a class consciousness (perverse or otherwise) in the gaming community in the years leading to the Global Great Recession. Adhering to anti-representational class concerns through commerce is the sure path to success in these titles, when success is measured against the symbolic order of action and possibility bearing on time as recorded in the player's inventory. One cannot experience exchange in *The Sims* or *The Sims Online* or *World of Warcraft* and avoid the significance of capital to class. Or, to use Bogost's concept, the procedural rhetoric of the games does not allow for the player to play beyond the bounds of class and market, even if the player decides to steer his or her avatar into surreal or mysterious representations. The observation is particularly relevant to Leeson, to the extent that it underscores a practical but unstated utility for the romantic "descent into poverty" for shooter titles, as well as potentially other titles and genres of play. The sense that the player is literally on his or her heels with regards to a stable economic position—one that would allow him or her the luxury of choice—is specific to the immediate exchange actions the player will take.

While these and other theories can be used to rationalize aspects of play, it is important to note the limits of the theory offered in this text with regards to the general potential of such rationalizations. The material conditions of play fall well beyond the scope of this project, which seeks only to rationalize one productive scheme (of perhaps many) for detecting the potential forms and functions—strange or otherwise—of wealth and the wealthy within videogames. Fortunately, there is an emerging body of criticism that is concerned with the material conditions of play and with the significance of these conditions to twenty-first-century experiences of wealth inequality. Nick Dyer-Witheford and Grieg de Peuter have established a meaningful contribution to this subject in *Games of Empire: Global Capitalism and Video Games*. They argue that "video games are a paradigmatic media of Empire—planetary, militarized hypercapitalism— and of some of the forces that are presently hampering planetary, militarized hypercapitalism."[17] It is a grand claim buttressed at various points with trenchant comments on the concept of empire by Michael Hardt and Antonio Negri, Deleuze and Guattari, and Michel Foucault among others. With respect to the interlocking theories of Galloway, Castronova, Leeson, Wark, and Bogost, the work is especially useful because of its careful attention to the development of real-world corporations (EA and Microsoft, most notably) and their contributions to the development of a range of novel concepts with exciting analytical potential: for example, "cognitive capital," "militainment," "ludocapitalism," and the emergence of a frightening new superstructure that is "revealing itself as a school for labor, an instrument of rulership, and a laboratory for the fantasies of advanced techno-capital."[18] Their vision casts the gamer as what amounts to a machine, following the new machine logic of procedural rhetoric with perhaps unintended (and likely uncontrollable) outcomes.

While the scope of this grand theory falls far beyond my own, an initial association with their work can be made by attending to the challenging conception of "narrative" that runs throughout their text. The work persists in the turn-of-the-millennium struggle to get specific about this term. For example, early on the authors use "story" as a synonym for narrative: that is, " . . . graphics and narrative. These images and stories came from a distinct tradition."[19] From then on, there are numerous instances of "narrative" (and also story), but none of these usages take the reader any closer to a specific definition for either term.[20] Indeed, the only discernible function is again the "tofu" function that is evident in Galloway or Castronova—that is, as an empty concept that is associated with some other qualifying term: narratives that have "established recognition," narratives that are "manifest content," and a narrative of "Marx's founding concept" are all identified at one point or another. What it is, exactly, that the authors are talking about when they talk about narratives or stories is far from clear. The notions that narrative is the expansion of a verb; that exchange for termination, continuation, and stasis have bearing on a spectrum of games; and that such bearing can be interpreted as a constructive force in those titles' symbolic orders of action and possibility bearing on time suggest a path forward for testing Dyer-Witheford and de Peuter's theories under specific conditions. And these theories should be tested, if for no other reason than that they come with massive implications for the arguments of Galloway, Castronova, Wark, and Bogost. For example, the authors associate the player's act of play with

> a massive twenty-first-century alteration in species-being rivaling in scale the changes generated by industrial capitalism, a metamorphosis that, if survivable, points perhaps to an unprecedented intensification of Empire, but also possibly to exodus from it. Virtual games are one molecular component of this undecidable collective mutation, which is revolutionizing life from the mines to the metaverse.[21]

This argument is as hyperbolic as Wark's, but it comes with the added benefit of specific details to flesh out the more extravagant claims, and in this way begs to actually be tested for its potential accuracy. If, for example, videogames and gaming are relevant to an "unprecedented intensification of Empire," then how might such relevance be understood in the context of sentimental romance?

Interestingly, Frye's theory indicates that there are some significant challenges on the horizon for the sentimental romance as a genre in videogames should the conditions explored in *Games of Empire* be accurate and relevant in daily and future life. Frye is very specific in his criticism of romance under empire and argues that the genre tends to flourish only on the fringes of such social structures as there is something vegetable about the romantic imagination (e.g., it needs room to grow).[22] Whether the growth of planetary capitalism will be asymmetrical and leave room for such future developments is beyond the scope of this book. However, what is decidedly less hypothetical and essentially in keeping with Dyer-Witheford and de Peuter's theory is the observation that many titles associated with the era of the Global Great Recession (a recession of planetary capitalism, it should be remembered!) are invested in advancements systems with specific, contextualized meaning, and such meaning often estranges the character from a stable sense of self through totalizing experiences of fanciful finance.

It is beyond the scope of this project to test this dimension of Dyer-Witheford and de Peuter's hypothesis, but it is within the scope to consider whether and how the concept of capital itself is represented within the contextualizing scheme of the sentimental romance. Key games with roots in the era of the Global Great Recession do appear to offer telling representations of wealth and the wealthy that speak the Dyer-Witheford and de Peuter's materials concerns, and in ways that are perceptible under the logic of the system at hand and the major theories identified so far. This work can begin with a consideration of *BioShock* (2007) and *Mass Effect* (2007).

With regards to Frye and Leeson, *BioShock* can be associated with the context of romance, proper sentimental romance, and literature. With regards to the context of romance, the game is composed of anti-representational people, places, and things in coincidental plot intersections. With regards to sentimental romance, it presents a truncated list of staid romantic hallmarks, most notably hallmarks of the underworld: a literal descent in the form of a crash into an underworld labyrinth populated with fertility and death spirits, organized in the service of an absurd ritual that literally calls the identity of "Jack" into question. With regards to literature, the game places notable weight on not just the descent to the underworld, but the significant social and psychological themes that bear on the player's efforts to ascend from that world back into something like a normal life. These categories are not meant to oversimplify the game, but they do allow for it to be called into a certain shape and critical order.

With regards to the concept of narrative that is significant to this project, *BioShock* provides the experience of exchange for termination, continuation, and stasis. Without reducing the broader possibilities for such exchange, specific examples for each category can be described as follows: Jack engages with the "splicers" of Rapture and terminates them to proceed. Jack exchanges action with set pieces (doors and walls) to continue his journey. With regards to stasis, he acquires in the literal form of currency exchange to remain adequate to his developing surroundings. While it is not the case that all possible exchange opportunities are necessary for the player to persist through the title, certain experiences from each of the categories must be completed for advancement to occur.

The late-in-the-game revelation that Jack has been pre-programmed to carry out any order delivered with the phrase "would you kindly" draws into sharp relief the actions that are necessary for the player to progress through the game, as well as actions that are informative of the player's collective, superficial experiences of exchange. Importantly, this distinction is entirely conceptual and affective with regards to the title's symbolic order of action and possibility bearing on time, which—as Bogost reminds us—is necessarily limited in games by a determining language (the procedural rhetoric) of the game itself. And this is precisely why this moment is so important with regards to the sentimental romance. The revelation affirms the sentimental romance's vision of the absurd in the underworld—and the capacity of such absurdity to determine the identity of the hero with a novel, totalizing context for the previously established symbolic order of action and possibility bearing on time. Such affirmation and its determining capacities hardly needs further explanation for any player familiar with sentimental romance, as the game has literally been a march through the ancient curves and contortions of this genre from the very beginning of play. For such players, the revelation of absurdity is not a moment of "estrangement" from the game, or of supposed "ludonarrative dissonance." No—it is a moment of genre fulfillment, specific to the instance of fulfillment: a predictable variable that is part and parcel of the ancient romantic scheme.

While the moment has implications for the player's actions, it has special relevance to the game's own version of capital: "Adam," the prime currency in Andrew Ryan's weird little empire. Insofar as the player's decision to harvest or not harvest Adam is framed as a moral choice, one with both immediate and long-term implications for play, the game pushes the experience of capital acquisition—which is a constant condition of play—into a distinct conceptual realm. The significance of that realm is perhaps of great or simply no consequence to the player, insofar as he or she wants to imagine the moral implications of the possible actions as being definitive of Jack's "identity." Nevertheless, it establishes a second order of play within the game. Like the optional ghost deaths in *Pac Man*, these moments come with attendant graphical and aesthetic concerns that are essentially superficial to play. While the player can avoid such opportunities to harvest Adam in the game from the Little Sisters, those actions and opportunities depend on exchange for termination—as the player must terminate the Little Sister's Big Daddy to have the experience in the first place. This is the structure of the illusion of choice in *BioShock*, and this illusion depends on the same exchange opportunities that are called into question and rendered absurd by the ritual of dominance that is revealed at the heart of Rapture. As variables with relevance to the symbolic order of action and possibility bearing on time, these are, for Levine, "the smallest bits of narrative"—or at least some of the smallest bits—that he is seeking in game design.

Wark's hypothetical gamer—situated in a subservient relationship with the game's procedural rhetoric (as determined by Bogost) is of course already in the position of being totally directed by the game prior to the revelation that "Jack" lacks free will. At the level of abstraction, then, the gamer's situation is like that of the hero of *BioShock*. However, as Galloway reminds us, that situation is actually far more complicated than this. The actual conditions of the real-world gamer's life are always significant. Consequently, if the gamer is to find any kind of personal resonance with Jack, a detailed rationale would need to emerge to explain that resonance. Castronova would unite the game and gamer over a common conception of capitalism, a notion that seems relevant enough given the gameplay opportunities to purchase goods from vending machines. However, the actual conditions of play underscore the triviality of such acts, as the casual disbursement of many forms of capital across the game affirms the absurd nature of wealth itself. The degenerate form of commerce in *BioShock* raises all kinds of questions about what wealth is in the game, where it comes from and who owns it—and insofar as that is true, the game approaches the concerns of Thomas Piketty's modern individual, who is constantly scrambling to acquire just enough wealth to persist but never enough to feel comfortable or secure in his or her holdings. The scenario becomes even more dramatic with the revelation of the absurd ritual, which lays bare the very act of wealth acquisition itself as occurring outside of Jack and the player's determining capacities: wealth and the wealthy are surreal and mysterious precisely because they distance Jack from a stable sense of self.

Like *BioShock, Mass Effect* can be associated with the context of romance, sentimental romance, and literature. At the level of context, the associations are essentially similar: anti-representational people, places, and things are drawn into convergence with coincidental plots. With regards to the concept of literature, these subjects are crucial for the various literal and symbolic forms of ascent and descent that the player experiences during play. Such action is of course literalized through the movements of spaceships, but it also has symbolic value in the player's descent into a vast conspiracy theory, and his or her efforts to rise from that world with the knowledge that is needed to save the galaxy. Along the way, there are many individuals and instances that can be associated with the logic of sentimental romance: adventures involving pirates of one sort or another, narrow escapes from death, and the recognition of the identity of the hero.[23] Like *BioShock* and many of the other games considered in this argument, the title plays out in what is generally a night world scenario.

Shepard's identity as the herald of the encroaching Reaper horde is affirmed in the absurd ritual of the Reaper invasion. This ritual, as such, constitutes the fundamental experience of *Mass Effect*'s night world scenario. One of the more notable aspects of this game is that, throughout, the player is presented with exchange opportunities for termination, continuation, and stasis with significance to his or her "advancement system." The system is relatively complex and records the player's acquisition of avatar capital—both in terms of goods and in terms of his or her developing personality. Within this system, there are innumerable potential paths for the player to trod before he or she comes to the game's essential conclusion—which may occur in a short range of forms, though they all end with essentially the same affirmation of the player's chosen identity as the correct herald of the Reapers absurd 50,000 year-long ritual of galactic destruction.

While this scenario has many, many more moving parts than the conclusion of, say, *Super Mario Brothers*, it is also true that in terms of the logic of sentimental romance it is essentially the same ending: identity is affirmed in relation to an absurd ritual. The appreciable difference is the complexity of the symbolic order of action and possibility bearing on time as represented in player inventory. Games have gone from points and stars and time to a dazzling array of variable gear features and other factors that are also recorded with chronological time: in *Mass Effect*, there is a time stamp on the player's "saved" game. These constraints are an indication that the romantic concerns of Mario are also relevant to Captain Shepard.

The contingency of Wark's gamer to the procedural rhetoric of *Mass Effect* is as significant to Galloway's claims as it is in the consideration of *BioShock*, insofar as the player's decisions for Shepard are assumedly intentional but constrained in significant ways by the title's possibilities for discourse. Here, too, Castronova has specific relevance, in the sense that capitalist values are certainly relevant to play: the player is provided with opportunities to not only purchase goods, but also to sell them. However, it is also the case that the weird disbursement of many of the same goods around the gamespace draws the values associated with such exchanges into question. Yet, capitalism itself shrinks before the existential horror of the Reapers (though admittedly it does help to win the day!) in the sense that the Reapers represent a fundamental threat to all life. With regards to the symbolic order of action and possibility bearing on time, Shepard's repulsion of the attack can occur under a dizzying array of equipment arrangements and personality settings, which has the effect of rendering wealth itself a variable in the service of the romantic climax. What does it mean to have wealth in *Mass Effect*? What does it mean to be wealthy? In ways that *Super Mario Brothers* does not precisely because its advancement system is far less ornate in comparison, *Mass Effect* underscores in significant ways the essential triviality of capital to the player's identity: Shepherd's options are so vast by comparison, and it is possible to reach the end of the game in any number of formulations.

However, and with special respect to Levine, it should be noted that the game is essentially zero-sum. For example, while it is true that the game allows for multiple paths to the conclusion, and while that conclusion can be impacted by player choice—the game can be said to be "zero sum" with respect to the combined relevance of those paths and choices to the title's concluding romantic gesture: which is to affirm whatever identity the player has crafted for Shepard in the context of an absurd ritual playing out in a night world scenario, one that affirms Shepard as the hero of the moment. This affirmation of the structure of sentimental romance is significant to the concept of capital in this game: the wealth possibilities escape conceptualization even as their functions align under a single gesture—a characterization of Shepard as Hero. This contradiction between kinds of wealth and their possible functions renders the very experience of cycling through wealth mysterious and surreal.

BioShock and *Mass Effect* each pair a relatively granular and complex capital system with a singular conception of identity. In either title, that identity is the inescapable product of a romantic scenario, subject to the detailing features of the player's acquisition "choices."

These situations are significant to the history of capital representations in videogames, insofar as they contribute to a series of romantic titles that associate a symbolic order of action and possibility bearing on time with an inventory system. Such associations constitute a determining feature of the player's act of play, insofar as play can be represented under a broad range of recorded values. The expansion of these systems from mere point tallies to inventories that reflect an ever-widening range of the player's gameplay decisions indicates an increased focus on capital and its acquisition as a prime feature of the sentimental romance in the videogame form. The essentially singular trajectory of the player character in these titles (with minor variations) indicates that such acquisition is in fact occurring in the service of romantic structures, which provide a clear and extremely limiting purpose for capital: the affirmation of the romantic hero, however he or she is construed within an absurd ritual. In this way, the representation of capital is working to affirm personal identity at a time—as Piketty reminds us—when the nature of capital has never been less certain for more people in the Western world, particularly with regards to its implications for personal identity. The desire for cultural affirmations of personal identity through mass media is, Joan Shelley Rubin argues, a decidedly American desire, and videogames are contributing to this established cultural concern in inventive ways in the new millennium.

CHAPTER 6

Conclusion: The Wealth of Virtual Nations

Abstract Crowley concludes with an affirmation of the limitations of his proposed program and outlines paths for future inquiry in subsequent considerations of wealth and capital in videogame narratives. Special attention is paid to potential applications of Genette's major theories to the videogame form as well as individual videogames. This work anticipates extended considerations of Frye's general literary theories and their bearing on videogames, generally—as well as specific considerations of the ways in which particular economic aspirations and anxieties can be associated with videogames from select periods and nations.

Keywords Thomas Piketty · Alexander Galloway · McKenzie Wark · Ian Bogost · Global Great Recession · *Spacewar!*

The identified program of analysis carries with it the conceptual limitations of its base assumptions: for example, its adopted definition for "narrative," its attention to acts of exchange with outcomes, and its association of these notions with the broad curves and contours of the sentimental romance. A rationale for the alignment of these concerns is offered with the expectation that the program has inherent values for the interpretation of the gamer and his or her act of play. However, it is also the case that the kinds of interpretations that are anticipated under this project also reside on a collection of theoretical observations that have their own individual and collective limitations. Frye and Genette's grand theories are of course contingent upon intertextual associations, which assume implicit or explicit efforts on the part of authors to orchestrate their works in intimate ways over vast stretches of time. A similar claim can be made about the work of Thomas Piketty, who charts the forces of convergence and divergence across the centuries as if their meaning is and has been fixed across the rise and fall of empires. These broad stroke assumptions are useful to the extent that they remain subject to perpetual skepticism, and for as long as they can withstand critique. Presently, evidence of their utility is widespread in academic circles. This may not always be the case.

In its findings, the program also reveals the contingency of its values for interpretation. Galloway and Castronova's assumptions that the videogame form provides the player with a unique opportunity to act has yet to be theorized to a point of general satisfaction, insofar as it assumes there is something passive about traditional prose media—a notion with which most readers with even a basic imagination would take exception. Moreover, Wark's positioning of the gamer as an individual out of time and place and Bogost's identification of a somehow novel "procedural rhetoric" in videogames should strike even the casual reader as extreme, given that no legitimate subject exists in perfect isolation, or in a state of contextual novelty. However, while the critic should expect the conceptual horizon offered by these arguments to fall away in an instant, the very enthusiasm these critics bring to their subjects is inspiration enough for scholars interested in this emerging field to charge ahead into the conditions that are responsible for such excitement.

The notion that there is something "here," something to a collection of game titles published in the millennial period that connects gamers to the broad and meaningful development of the Western world is powerful enough to pursue even under unsure conditions. As Joan Shelley Rubin reminds her readers, Americans of modest means have long aspired to emulate the lives they find in popular fictions. At their best or worst, these are the stories that set "the scene" for many North Americans, in terms of their capacities to imagine an inherently valuable future self, one that is not degraded in all the ways one is likely to be degraded in a capitalist system defined by the day-to-day challenges of extreme wealth inequality. At their worst, such notions may be naive—but even naiveté can be a noble sentiment when it emerges as an alternative to otherwise unavoidable despair. This has, of course, always been a prime function of the sentimental romance, which Frye identifies as a genre that has emerged as one effort to pull the chaos of daily life into a certain, tolerable order.[1] The image of millions of Americans endlessly playing videogames in the basements of homes under foreclosure in the new millennium calls this situation to mind and gives it added poignancy.

The argument has pursued something like a linear explanation for the development of sentimental romance and has operated under the logic that early titles have a significant investment in the context of romance, and that such investments laid the conceptual foundation for later, more complicated titles. While it is possible to chart a logical series of developments from *Spacewar!* to *Mass Effect* in the service of such notions, the complexity of the field and the very early emergence of titles with the essential structure of sentimental romance (e.g., *The Oregon Trail*), should throw into doubt the assumption that there is a single shining path along which videogames have marched towards a more "fully developed" form. Moreover, the fact that many of the titles considered in this project have had a remarkable presence in the market at the expense of other works should underscore the contingency of their relevance to the larger argument and can lead to questions about alternative titles. Consequently, the rationale that connects each of these chapters is offered only as a rationale in the service of the argument's basic propositions, not as the rationale that is necessitated by either the propositions or the vast catalogue of potential titles. The notion is particularly important, given the stated objections to Piketty's own brand of literary analysis, which makes significant points but which is undone by the author's extraordinary and essentially unwarranted surety of the appropriateness of his own examples to his broader project.

Of all the propositions in the offered logic, perhaps the most crucial are those that relate to rhetoric and context. The notion that *Spacewar!*, a title initially made simply to entertain a small group of well-educated players who were conversant with then-contemporary works of pulp science fiction, would have gameplay features that would find vast acceptance across enormous numbers of people is fascinating. On the one hand, the argument seems to support Frye's notion that there is something about the context of romance itself that stimulates the essential human imagination.[2] On the other hand, it raises questions about what it was that may have been going on around videogames at the time of their insertion into the culture that facilitated their popularity. Rubin's work establishes a useful context for the acceptance of mass media in the decades prior to the emergence of the videogame form, and it is true that this project has not considered this subject as it relates to the emergence of videogames, which is notable for several reasons, most significantly of course because the argument spends so much time insisting that the Global Great Recession is crucial to the player's act of play in the contemporary world.

Another direction for future work, then, could consider the socioeconomic conditions of videogame narratives, from their production to dissemination, to their transformation under various kinds of players across time. While the project at hand could surely benefit from greater attention to this subject, it has been crucial to first establish a conceptual standard for such investigations. The need for a stable standard is evident when the work of Wark and Bogost is considered: without taking anything away from either author's investigations, they both operate (quite admirably!) under the twin tasks of defining a field at the same moment they construct their own unique tool sets for ascertaining their chosen horizons. The work is often quite good, but it is also quite insular to the extent that its rationalizations are either generated on the spot or woven together with great speed from a grab-bag of critical positions with as-of-yet undefined relevance to the subject or subjects at hand, as well as to each other. Are we really to believe that Adorno and Plato stare at each other from across the centuries and see eye-to-eye, over a subject as contested as "narrative"? No, of course not—or at least not yet, but I am certainly open to a good argument in that vein. Moreover, such insularity positions either theorist as a point of origin for future study, a position that may be more or less reasonable, but it should not come at the expense of the old models for seeing and knowing. It is important to remember that Plato's vision already leads out of the Cave, and that Socrates's discussion of *diegesis* emerges as part of a broader interpretive system, the relevance of which to the modern world has not yet been disproven by another Socrates.

And the old models are indeed useful! Genette's attention to verbal structures sets the stage for a massive set of interpretive possibilities, each awaiting its own rationalization. However, it is also the case that Genette's scheme does not indicate a potential value for those components beyond its own categories. The concept of sentimental romance, linked under Frye's notion that narratives constitute a verbal structure, has special value to the limits of Genette's contemplations insofar as it allows for an interpretation and potential alignment of Genette's verbal developments with the catalogue of romantic units that Frye associates with sentimental romance. Here, then, is where *Spacewar!* becomes something more than an exercise in exchange for termination, and *Pac Man* more than a demonstration of exchange for termination or continuation. They become evidence of the still-beating heart of the romantic imagination and its relevance to twenty-first-century narratives.

This is also a moment to reflect on how such analysis can work to rescue the videogame form from too basic definitions. For example, while Galloway considers the videogame as a subject that enables interactivity, it is also true that the concept of interactivity is so general as to have any range of meanings: for example, physical, intellectual, imaginative, and so on. This is not to say that the essential notion is incorrect, only that it raises questions about the kinds of experiences that are relevant to the definition. Thus, without invalidating Galloway's definition, it can be argued that media should be assessed for their narratives—that is, their demonstrated verbal developments—rather than for their conceptual boundaries. What is the value in attempting to summarize the potential of "the book" or "the map" if one is speaking of narratives delivered through books, or narratives delivered through maps? Such pursuits are not illogical, but they would seem to mistake the contours of the forest for the possible trees that might be found within the forest.

Another way to view the question of how (or whether) the videogame form should be defined is to reflect on the last decade or so of videogame scholarship, which offers a great deal—but which also speaks to general and widespread confusion over the question of narrative. Lacking anything like a productive movement for the consideration of this subject, it is hard to imagine that the field is at all ready to step forward with a definition for the assumedly much more specific subject of the videogame form. However, before critics start building astrolabes to determine the videogame form and its base possibilities, it is important to remember that the question of form—at least at the level of denotation—has limited value in many humanist pursuits. What is a novel? What is a poem? What is a painting? A materialist answer can be derived, but how satisfying is it likely to be, given that the arts are defined by media manipulations, transformations, and outright inversions undertaken in efforts to constantly test and redefine the limits of form. Thus, the question of form is significant, and the history of forms is always relevant, but a determinist stance on form has all the longevity of a grocery list for an ailing pet.

The sentimental romance provides an excellent path for respecting contemporary efforts to understand the videogame form in the productive context of an age-old genre. Such considerations do require that the genre itself be included in analysis—that is, one must begin from the assumption that there is relevance, and before one can come to that conclusion one must of course know what the sentimental romance is and (most importantly) have a certain level of investment in the cultural conditions that have propelled the genre across human time and spaces. Thus, the critic must be, if not a humanist, at least conversant with humanism as a pre-existing social context for the videogame form.

NOTES

CHAPTER 1

1. Piketty, *Capital*, 259.
2. Leeson, "Northrop Frye and the Story Structure of the Single-Player Shooter."
3. Galloway, "Social Realism in Gaming," http://www.gamestudies.org/0401/galloway/.
4. Ibid.
5. Castronova, *Synthetic Worlds*, chap. 8.
6. Ibid.
7. Amber Davisson and Danielle Ghem, "Gaming Citizenship: Video Games as Lessons in Civic Life," 44.
8. Marcus Schulzke, "The Virtual Culture Industry: Work and Play in Virtual Worlds," 21.
9. Castronova, *Exodus*, chap. 5.
10. Wark, *Gamer Theory*, chap. "Agony (of the Cave)."
11. Ibid., chap. "Battle (on Rez)."
12. Bogost, *Persuasive Games*, chap. 8.
13. Ibid., chap. Preface.
14. Paul Krugman, "Why We're in a New Gilded Age," http://www.nybooks.com/articles/2014/05/08/thomas-piketty-new-gilded-age/.
15. Janet H. Murray, "The Last Word on Ludology v Narratology," https://inventingthemedium.com/2013/06/28/the-last-word-on-ludology-v-narratology-2005/.
16. Genette, *Fiction and Diction*, 11.

© The Author(s) 2017
A. Crowley, *The Wealth of Virtual Nations*,
DOI 10.1007/978-3-319-53246-2

17. Ibid., *Narrative Discourse: An Essay in Method*, 30.
18. Torodov, *Grammaire*, 10.
19. Rimmon-Kenan, *Narrative*, 143.
20. Herman, *New Perspectives*, 1–3.
21. Ibid., 2.
22. Flundernik, "Histories," 46.
23. Nünning, "Narratology," 239–75.
24. Herman, "Histories," 19–35.
25. Barbara Herrnstein Smith, "Narrative Versions, Narrative Theories," 213–14.
26. Murray, "The Last Word." https://inventingthemedium.com/2013/06/28/the-last-word-on-ludology-v-narratology-2005/.
27. Hocking, "Ludonarrative Dissonance in *Bioshock*." http://clicknothing.typepad.com/click_nothing/2007/10/ludonarrative-d.html.
28. Frasca, "Ludology Meets Narratology: Similitude and Differences Between (video)games and Narrative," http://www.ludology.org/articles/ludology.htm.
29. Murray, "The Last Word," https://inventingthemedium.com/2013/06/28/the-last-word-on-ludology-v-narratology-2005/.
30. Genette, *Narrative Discourse: An Essay in Method*, 25–32.
31. Genette, *Fiction and Diction*, 78.
32. Hocking, "Ludonarrative," http://clicknothing.typepad.com/click_nothing/2007/10/ludonarrative-d.html.
33. Levine, "Narrative Legos," http://www.gdcvault.com/play/1020434/Narrative.
34. Ibid.
35. Levine, "Narrative Legos," http://www.gdcvault.com/play/1020434/Narrative.
36. Piketty, *Capital*, 323.
37. Ibid., 50–57.
38. Ibid., 265.

CHAPTER 2

1. Piketty, *Capital*, 105–06.
2. Ibid., 2.
3. Ibid.
4. Campbell, 183.
5. Cook, 1.
6. Piketty, *Capital*, 53.

7. Ibid., 102.
8. Ibid., 106.
9. Ibid., 110.
10. Ibid., 412.
11. Ibid., 379.
12. Ibid., 46.
13. Ibid., 114.
14. Ibid., 152.
15. Ibid., 259.
16. Rubin, *Middlebrow*, chap. "Introduction."
17. Ibid., 2.
18. Rubin, *Middlebrow*, 1.
19. Ibid., 2.
20. Ibid., 4.
21. Ibid., 3.
22. Ibid., 14.
23. Ibid., 16–17.
24. Ibid., 330.
25. Frye, *The Secular Scripture*, 97.
26. Ibid., 3–4.
27. Ibid., 104.
28. Ibid., 4.
29. Ibid., 6.
30. Ibid., 36.
31. Ibid., 7.
32. Ibid., 97.
33. Ibid., 53.
34. Leeson, "Northrop Frye and the Story Structure of the Single-Player Shooter,"137.
35. Ibid., 145.
36. Frye, *The Secular Scripture*, 44.
37. Ibid., 1.
38. Ibid., 4.
39. Ibid., 5.
40. Donovan, *Replay*, 9–10.
41. Frye, *The Secular Scripture*, 15.
42. Ibid., 10.
43. Ibid., 3.
44. Rubin, *Middlebrow*, 329–30.

CHAPTER 3

1. Frye, *The Secular Scripture*, 17.
2. Ibid., 26.
3. Genette, *Narrative Discourse, 30.*
4. Frye, *The Secular Scripture*, chap. 2.
5. Ibid., 97.
6. Ibid., 98.
7. Leeson, "Northrop Frye and the Story Structure of the Single-Player Shooter."
8. Frye, *The Secular Scripture*, chap. 4.
9. Atari. *Pac-Man.* https://atariage.com/manual_html_page.php?SoftwareLabelID=342.
10. Nintendo, "*Super Mario Bros.* Instruction Booklet." http://legendsofloca lization.com/media/super-mario-bros/manuals/Super-Mario-Bros-Manual-US.pdf.
11. Ibid.
12. Frye, *The Secular Scripture*, chap. 1.
13. Ibid.
14. Galloway, "Social Realism in Gaming," http://www.gamestudies.org/0401/galloway/.
15. Nintendo, "*Super Mario Bros.* Instruction Booklet," http://legendsofloca lization.com/media/super-mario-bros/manuals/Super-Mario-Bros-Manual-US.pdf.
16. Sega, "*Sonic the Hedgehog* Instruction Manual," http://info.sonicretro.org/images/b/bb/Sonic1_MD_US_SonicJam_manual.pdf#page=1.
17. Nintendo, "*Donkey Kong Country* Instruction Booklet," http://www.gamesdatabase.org//Media/SYSTEM/Nintendo_SNES/Manual/for mated/Donkey_Kong_Country_-_1994_-_Nintendo.pdf.
18. Sony, "*Crash Bandicoot* Instruction Manual," http://www.gamesdatabase.org/Media/SYSTEM/Sony_Playstation//Manual/formated/Crash_Bandicoot_-_1996_-_Sony_Computer_Entertainment.pdf.
19. Genette, *Narrative Discourse*, 244–45.
20. Ibid., 31–32.
21. Frye, *The Secular Scripture*, chap. 1
22. Anderson, *Imagined Communities*, 53.
23. Frye, *The Secular Scripture and Other Writings on Critical Theory*, chap. 16.
24. Frye, *The Secular Scripture*, 4.
25. Frye, *The Secular Scripture*. chap. 4.
26. Rubin, Making of Middle Brow, chap. "Introduction."

Chapter 4

1. Galloway, "Social Realism in Gaming," http://www.gamestudies.org/ 0401/galloway/.
2. Ibid.
3. Ibid.
4. Ibid.
5. Frye, *The Secular Scripture*, 7.
6. Galloway, "Social Realism in Gaming," http://www.gamestudies.org/ 0401/galloway/.
7. Castronova, *Synthetic Worlds*, chap. 4., chap. 8, chap. "Notes."
8. Ibid., chap. "Notes."
9. Ibid., chap.1.
10. Ibid.
11. Ibid., chap. 4.
12. Ibid.
13. Castronova, *Synthetic Worlds*, chap. 7.
14. Leeson, "Northrop Frye and the Story Structure of the Single-Player Shooter," 137–52.
15. Frye, *The Secular Scripture*, 3.

Chapter 5

1. Wark, *Gamer Theory*, chap. "Battle."
2. Ibid., chap. "Endnotes."
3. Ibid, chap. "Cuts."
4. Ibid.
5. Ibid.
6. Ibid., chap. "Agony (or the Cave)."
7. Bogost, *Persuasive Games*, chap. "Preface."
8. Ibid.
9. Stephen Halliwell, "Diegesis—Mimesis," *The Living Handbook of Narratology*, http://lhn.uni-hamburg.de.
10. Bogost, *Persuasive Games*, chaps. "Procedural Rhetoric," "Political Processes," "Ideological Frames," "Learning," "Notes."
11. Genette, *Narrative*, 26.
12. Bogost, *Persuasive Games*, chap. "Procedural Rhetoric."
13. Ibid., chap. "Political Processes."
14. Wark, *Gamer Theory*, chap. "Agony (of The Cave."
15. Ibid.

16. Castronova, *Exodus*, chap. 3.
17. Nick Dyer-Witheford and Grieg de Peuter, *Global*, 167.
18. Ibid., 241.
19. Ibid., 15.
20. Ibid., 15, 36, 45, 92, 125, 161, 163, 176, 180, 195, 221, 235, 256, 269.
21. Ibid., 230.
22. Frye, *The Secular Scripture and Other Writings on Critical Theory*, chap. 16.
23. Frye, *The Secular Scripture*, 4.

CHAPTER 6

1. Frye, *The Secular Scripture*, 31.
2. Ibid., 36.

BIBLIOGRAPHY

A Force More Powerful. Washington, DC: BreakAway Games, 2006.

America's Army. United States Army, 2002.

Anderson, Benedict. *Imagined Communities: Reflections on the Origins and Spread of Asteroids.* Sunnyvale: Atari, 1979.

Bioshock. Boston: Infinite Games, 2007.

BioShock Infinite. Boston: Infinite Games, 2013.

Bogost, Ian. *Persuasive Games: The Expressive Power of Videogames.* Cambridge: MIT Press, 2007. Kindle edition

Campbell, David. "The Fetishism of Divergence: A Critique of Piketty." *Journal of Corporate Law Studies* 15, no. 1 (April 2015): 183–216.

Castronova, Edward. *Exodus to The Virtual World: How Online Fun is Changing Reality.* New York: Palgrave Macmillan, 2007.

Castronova, Edward. *Synthetic Worlds: The Business and Culture of Online Games.* Chicago: The University of Chicago Press, 2005. Kindle edition.

Castronova, Edward. *Wildcat Currency.* New Haven: Yale University Press, 2014.

Centipede. Sunnyvale: Atari, 1980.

Chatman, Seymour. *Story and Discourse: Narrative Structure in Fiction and Film.* Ithaca: Cornell University Press, 1978.

Civilization. Mount Valley: MicroProse, 1991.

Cool, Eli. "The Progress and Poverty of Thomas Piketty." *Raritan* 35, no. 2 (Fall 2015): 1–19.

Crash Bandicoot. Instruction Manual. Tokyo: Sony PlayStation, 1996.

DarkWatch. San Diego: High Moon Studios, 2005.

© The Author(s) 2017
A. Crowley, *The Wealth of Virtual Nations*,
DOI 10.1007/978-3-319-53246-2

Davisson, Amber, and Danielle Ghem. "Gaming Citizenship: Video Games as Lessons I Civic Life." *Journal of Contemporary Rhetoric* 4, no. 3/4 (2014): 39–57.

Diablo. Irvine: Blizzard, 1996.

Donkey Kong Country. Kyoto: Nintendo, 1994.

Donkey Kong Country Instruction Manual. Kyoto: Nintendo, 1994.

Donovan, Tristan. *Replay*. Lewes: Yellow Ant, 2010. Kindle edition.

Doom 3. Mesquite: Id Software, 2004.

Dyer-Witheford, Nick and de Peuter, Greg. *Games of Empire: Global Capitalism and Video Games*. Minneapolis: University of Minnesota Press, 2009.

Everquest. Tokyo: Sony Online Entertainment, 1999.

F.E.A.R. Kirkland: Monolith Productions, 2005.

Flundernik, Monika. "Histories of Narrative Theory (II): From Structuralism to the Present." *A Companion to Narrative Theory*, 36–59. ed. James Phelan. Blackwell: Malden 2005.

Frasca, Gonzalo. "Ludology Meets Narratology: Similitude and Differences between (Video) Games and Narrative." *Ludoloy.org*. 1999: http://www.ludol ogy.org/articles/ludology.htm.

Frye, Northrop. "Myth as the Matrix of Literature." *Georgia Review*, 38 (Fall 1984): 465–76.

Frye, Northrop. *The Secular Scripture: A Study of the Structure of Romance*. Cambridge: Harvard University Press, 1978.

Frye, Northrop. *The Secular Scripture and Other Writings on Critical Theory: 1976–1991 Vol 18*, ed. Joseph Adamson and Jean Wilson. Toronto: University of Toronto Press, 2006. Kindle edition.

Galexian. Tokyo: Namco, 1979.

Galloway, Alexander R. "Social Realism in Gaming." *Game Studies* 4, no. 1 (November 2004): http://www.gamestudies.org/0401/galloway/.

Genette, Gérard. *Fiction and Diction*. Translated by Catherine Porter. Ithaca: Cornell University Press, 1993.

Genette, Gérard. *Narrative Discourse: An Essay in Method*. Translated by Jane E. Lewin. Ithaca: Cornell UP, 1980.

Gotcha. Sunnvale: Atari, 1973.

Gran Track 10. Sunnyvale: Atari, 1975.

Half-Life 2. Bellevue: Valve, 2004.

Halliwell, Stephen. "Diegesis – Mimesis." *The Living Handbook of Narratology*. ed. Peter Hühn. Hamburg: Hamburg University. http://www.lhn.uni-ham burg.de.

Halo 2. Bellevue: Bungie, 2004.

Halo: Combat Evolved. Bellevue: Bungie, 2001.

Herman, David. "Histories of Narrative Theory (I): A Genealogy of Early Developments." *A Companion to Narrative Theory*, 19–35. ed. James Phelan. Blackwell: Malden, 2005.

Herman, David, ed. *Narratologies: New Perspectives on Narrative Analysis.* Columbus: Ohio State University Press, 1999.

Hocking, Clint. "Ludonarrative Dissonance in *Bioshock.*" *Click Nothing.* 2007: http://clicknothing.typepad.com/click_nothing/2007/10/ludonarrative-d.html.

Kapell, Matthew Wilhelm, ed. *The Play Versus Story Divide in Game Studies: Critical Essays.* Jefferson: McFarland, 2016. Kindle edition.

Killzone. Tokyo: Sony Interactive Entertainment, 2004.

Kreiswirth, Martin. "Narrative Turn in the Humanities." *Routledge Encyclopedia of Narrative Theory*, 377–82. ed. David Herman. London: Routledge, 2005.

Krugman, Paul, "Why We're in a New Guilded Age." http://www.nybooks.com/articles/2014/05/08/thomas-piketty-new-gilded-age/.

Leeson, David M. "Northrop Frye and the Story Structure of the Single-Player Shooter." *ESC* 37, no. 2 (June 2011): 137–52.

Levine, Ken. "Narrative Legos." http://GDCvault.com. 2014: http://www.gdcvault.com/play/1020434/Narrative.

Mass Effect. Edmonton: BioWare, 2007.

Max Payne. Espoo: Remedy Entertainment, 2001.

Max Payne 2. New York City: Rockstar Games, 2003.

McKenzie, Wark. *Gamer Theory.* Cambridge: Harvard University Press, 2007. Kindle edition.

Middle-earth: Shadow of Mordor. Kirkland: Monolith Productions, 2014.

Murray, Janet H. "The Last Word on Ludology V Narratology." *Inventing the Medium.* 2005. https://inventingthemedium.com/2013/06/28/the-last-word-on-ludology-v-narratology-2005/.

Nünning, Ansgar. "Narratology or Narratologies? Taking Stock of Recent Developments, Critique and Modest Proposals for Future Usages of the Term." *What is Narratology? Questions and Answers Regarding the Status of a Theory*, 239–75. ed. Tom Kindt. Berlin: Walter de Gruyter, 2003.

Ortiz-Robles, Mario. "Local Speech, Global Acts: Performative Violence and the Novelization of the World." *Comparative Literature* 59, no. 1 (Winter 2007): 1–22.

Pac Man. Chicago: Midway, 1980.

Painkiller. Warsaw: People Can Fly, 2004.

Piketty, Thomas. *Capital in The Twenty-First Century.* Translated by Arthur Goldhammer. Cambridge: Harvard University Press, 2014.

Pong. Sunnyvale: Atari, 1972.

Quake 4. Mesquite: Id Software, 2005.

Rimmon-Kenan, Shlomith. *Narrative Fiction: Contemporary Poetics.* London: Routledge Methuen, 1983.

Schulzke, Marcus. "The Virtual Culture Industry: Work and Play in Virtual Worlds." *The Information Society*, no. 30: 20–30. doi: 10.1080/01972243.2013.855689.

Shelley Rubin, Joan. *The Making of Middlebrow Culture.* Chapel Hill: University of North Carolina Press, 1992. Kindle edition.

Smith, Barbara Herrnstein. "Narrative Versions, Narrative Theories." *Critical Inquiry* 7, no. 1 (Autumn 1980): 213–36.

SOCOM. Redmond: Zipper Interactive, 2002.

Sonic the Hedgehog. Tokyo: Sega, 1991.

Sonic the Hedgehog Instruction Manual. Tokyo: Sega, 1991.

Space Race. Sunnyvale: Atari, 1975.

Space Wars. El Cajon: Cinematronics, 1977.

Space Invaders. Chicago: Midway, 1978.

Spacewar!. Boston: Steve Russell, 1962.

Special Forces. Mount Valley: MicroProse, 1991.

Stanzel, F.K. *A Theory of Narrative.* New York: Cambridge University Press, 1986.

State of Emergency. New York City: Rock Star Games, 2002.

Super Mario Brothers. Kyoto: Nintendo, 1985.

Super Mario Bros. Instruction Booklet. Kyoto: Nintendo, 1985.

The Elder Scrolls: Arena. Rockville: Bethesda Softworks, 1994.

The Oregon Trail. Brooklyn Center: MECC, 1974.

The Sims. Redwood City: Electronic Arts, 2000.

The Sims Online. Redwood City: Electronic Arts, 2002.

The Suffering. Chicago: Midway Games, 2004.

Thief. Tokyo: Square Enix, 2014.

Todorov, Tzvetan. *Grammaire du Décaméron.* Mouton: The Hague, 1969.

Toywar. Etoy: Switzerland, 1999.

Under Ash. Dal al-Fikr, 2001.

World of Warcraft. Irvine: Blizzard, 2004.

INDEX

© The Author(s) 2017
A. Crowley, *The Wealth of Virtual Nations*,
DOI 10.1007/978-3-319-53246-2